Native Plant GARDENING FOR BIRDS, BEES & BUTTERFLIES
Rocky Mountains

George Oxford Miller

DEDICATION

This book is dedicated to my wife and life companion, Carole Price. Together we explored the wild places, wildlife, countries, and cultures of every continent except Antarctica. She has stood beside me with encouragement for all my projects, and her never-failing love gives me strength as I approach the final adventure we all must face.

ACKNOWLEDGMENTS

This book is but one additional step built on the decades-long efforts of numerous individuals and organizations who champion landscaping with native plants to remediate the environmental damage caused by human development.

O Friend!

In the garden of thy heart plant naught but the rose of love.

—Bahá'u'lláh, founder of the Bahá'í Faith

Cover and book design by Jonathan Norberg
Edited by Brett Ortler and Jenna Barron
Proofread by Emily Beaumont
ADK branding background by **chyworks/Shutterstock.com**
All cover photos by George Oxford Miller unless otherwise noted.
(Front cover) broomweed/snakeweed: **Jerrold James Griffith/shutterstock.com;** bee on alpine aster: **Lipatova Maryna/shutterstock.com;** western tanager: **M. Leonard Photography/shutterstock.com;** Palos Verdes blue butterfly; **shakedn/shutterstock.com;** blue background western tanager: **detchana wangkheeree/shutterstock.com;** Colorado blue columbine: **Sean Xu/shutterstock.com**
(Back cover) goldenrod background (top): **LutsenkoLarissa/shutterstock.com;** serviceberry: **Madlen/shutterstock.com;** wild bluebell: **Soho A Studio/shutterstock.com;** blue-eyed grass: **Sean Xu/shutterstock.com;**

10 9 8 7 6 5 4 3 2 1

Native Plant Gardening for Birds, Bees & Butterflies: Rocky Mountains
Copyright © 2024 by George Oxford Miller
Published by Adventure Publications
An imprint of AdventureKEEN
310 Garfield Street South
Cambridge, Minnesota 55008
(800) 678-7006
www.adventurepublications.net
All rights reserved
Printed in the United States of America
LCCN 2023052830 (print); 2023052831 (ebook)
ISBN 978-1-64755-439-2 (pbk.); ISBN 978-1-64755-440-8 (ebook)

Table of Contents

Dedication 2

Acknowledgments 2

Introduction 4

Why Plant a Pollinator Garden? 4
- Gardening in the Multi-Habitats of the Rocky Mountains 6
- Life Zones 7

Before You Plant: Create a Master Plan 9

Soil: Minerals, Nutrients & Air 10
- Precious Water, Poor Soils 11

Gardening from the Ground Up . . . 12

Weed or Wildflower? 12

ABCs for a Pollinator Habitat Garden 14

Selecting Plants 15
- Planting Using Plant Syndromes 16

The Basics of Plant Anatomy 18
- Flowers 18
- Flower Clusters 18
- Leaves 19

Urban Wildlife 20

Embracing Our Biological Heritage 20

Meet the Pollinators 21
- Bees 21
- Butterflies 22
- Moths 22
- Flies 23
- Beetles 24
- Birds 24

How to Use This Book 25

Rocky Mountain Plants at a Glance 25

Rocky Mountain Native Plants

Trees 38

Shrubs 52

Wildflowers 106

Vines & Groundcovers 232

Grasses 250

Garden Plants for Butterflies 260

Garden Plants for Bees 262

Container Garden for Pollinators 264

Bird Food & Nesting Plants 266

Hummingbird Plants 267

Larval Host List (By Butterfly/Moth Species) 268

Retail Sources of Rocky Mountain Native Seeds & Plants 271

Native Plant Societies 272

Botanical Gardens & Arboretums 273

Index 274

Photo Credits 277

About the Author 280

Introduction

In 1991, when I published my first book on landscaping with the native plants of the Southwest, the emphasis was on replacing thirsty exotic ornamentals with water-wise native plants adapted to survive local climate extremes. In the intervening decades, native plant advocates have emphasized reducing maintenance costs and creating a sense of place that embraces each region's unique biological heritage. Lady Bird Johnson, founder of the National Wildflower Center, famously said, "Florida should look like Florida and Texas look like Texas."

The beginning of the 21st century has witnessed an alarming increase in environmental destruction by urban sprawl, industrial expansion, global scale pollution, and planet-wide climate change. Pollinators have been hit particularly hard, with some regions losing up to 80% of insect numbers and diversity. Now, a major emphasis in native plant landscaping is to mitigate the habitat lost by our human activities. A pollinator garden will help repair our local environment one yard at a time.

Why Plant a Pollinator Garden?

The complex relationships in nature can fill us with a deep sense of mystery and even magic. You can look into the starry night sky and feel either insignificant in the scope of the universe, or thrill at being a part of the vast majestic cosmos. You can get the same feeling in your backyard when you see a butterfly or bee dancing from flower to flower sipping nectar and gathering pollen.

From our backyards to the tropical rainforests, the complex web that sustains life on the planet depends on native pollinators. Globally, insects pollinate nearly 80% of all flowering plants. Closer to home, pollinators fertilize 75% of all human food crops—the fruits, vegetables, and nuts we eat. In our backyard gardens, tomatoes, squash, peppers, fruit trees, and flowers all depend on pollinators.

Yet across the planet, the population of all insects is plummeting radically year by year. One overriding reason is that human activities have significantly altered 75% of the planet's landmass. Forty percent of the natural area in the continental United States has been altered, including 59% in the Midwest and 47% in the South. With the Mountain West's burgeoning population, pristine plant and animal communities that have evolved together since the last Ice Age are being replaced by sprawling cities, suburbs, industrial farms, and energy development.

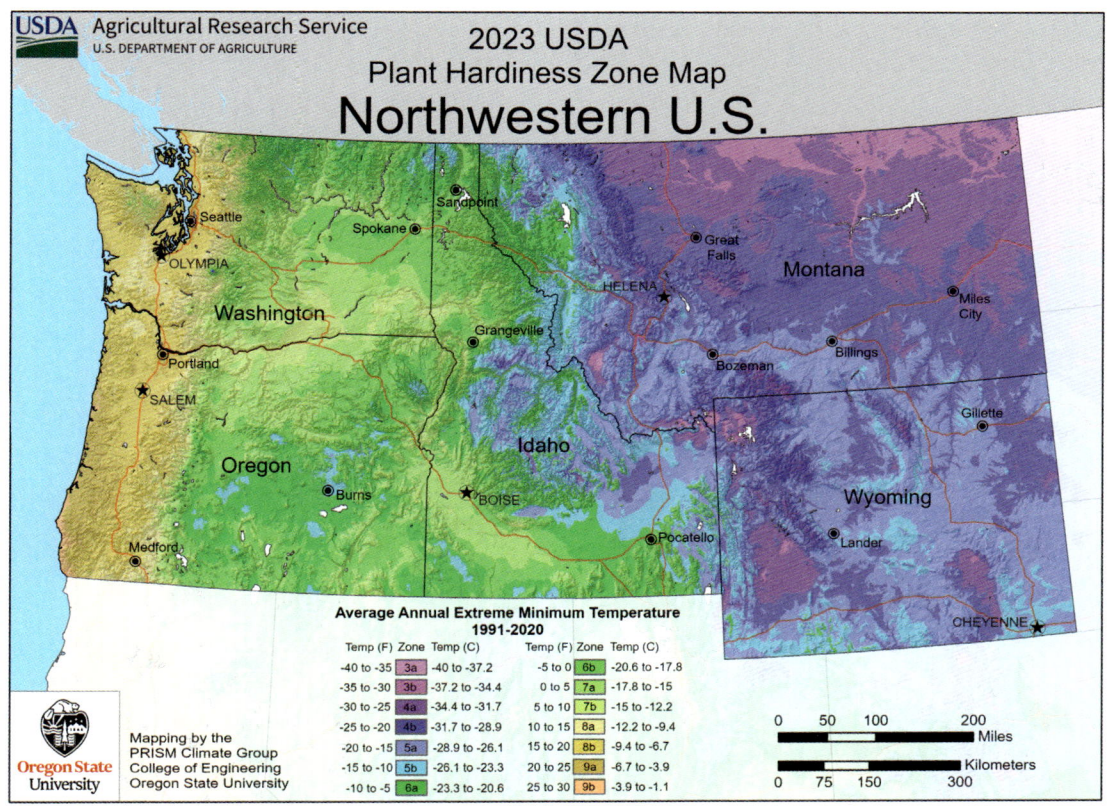

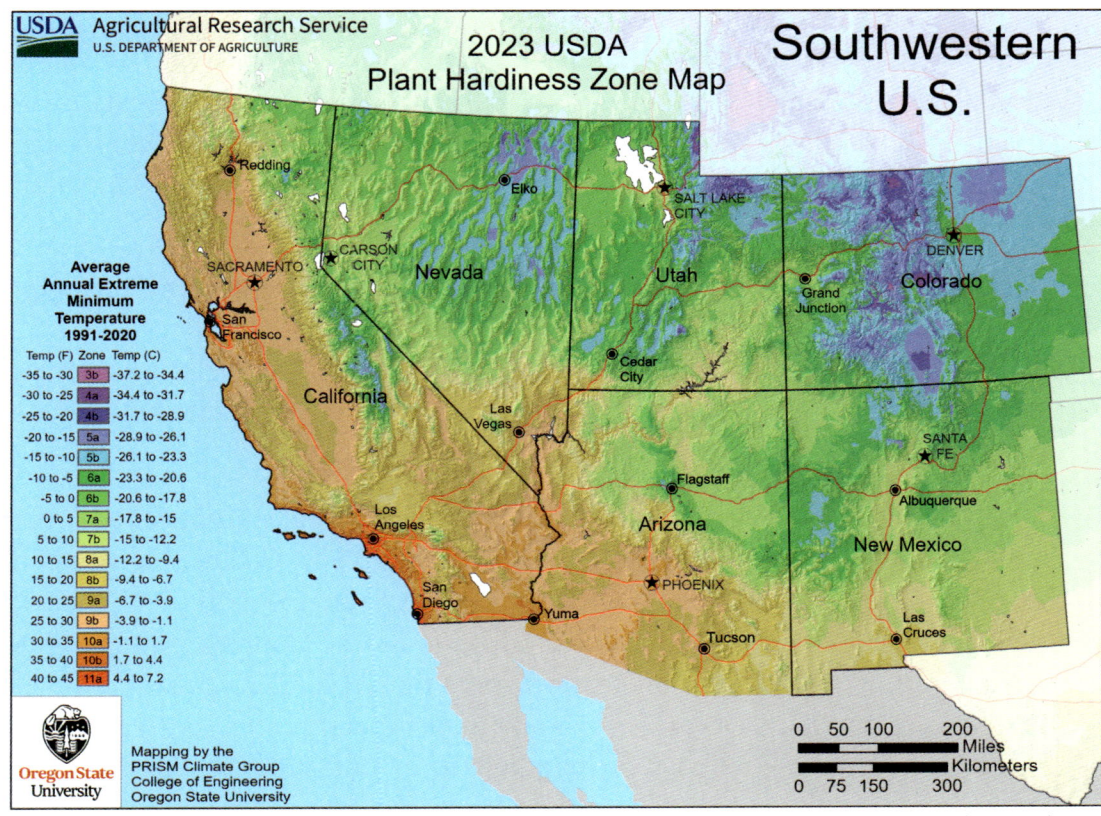

Credit: *USDA Plant Hardiness Zone Map for Northwestern US and Southwestern US,* 2023. Agricultural Research Service, US Department of Agriculture. Accessed from planthardiness.ars.usda.gov.

A significant portion of the natural habitat sacrificed for urban expansion is replaced by homes, businesses, and public medians and roadsides, much of which are landscaped with exotic grasses and invasive wildflowers and shrubs from other parts of the world. For native pollinators, such landscapes offer about as much sustenance as an asphalt parking lot. The simple fact is that to survive, native pollinators need native plants.

What good will a small backyard garden do to help sustain local pollinator populations? You will be pleasantly surprised! Wildlife in the Rockies live in what ecologists call a "patchy environment." Butterflies, bees, birds, and other pollinators forage over large areas, depending on their mobility, to find often-ephemeral patches of food, water, shelter, and nesting sites. Spotty thunderstorms may stimulate a shrubland of foothill mass bloom that only lasts a week or so. Snow runoff triggers a temporary bloom of talus, tundra, and meadow wildflowers, while a perennial spring may support a small, summer-long succession of blooms.

Many of the temporary oases that pollinators frequent on their daily foraging routes are no larger than the average backyard. But our yards can be better than a here-today, gone-tomorrow stopover. The greater gardening goal goes beyond planting a patch of pretty flowers, though that's certainly commendable in itself. It encompasses the long-term development of a backyard mini-refuge, a wildlife habitat that supplies the food, water, shelter, and nesting sites that butterflies, bees, and birds require to support a year-round sustainable population.

Gardens start with a dream and build into a passion. This book will help you create a pollinator garden encompassing a diversity of plants with a variety of sizes and shapes, and with plants that bloom from early spring to late fall. So, literally, grab your spade. "Plant it and they will come."

Wildflowers near Vail, Colorado

GARDENING IN THE MULTI-HABITATS OF THE ROCKY MOUNTAINS

Designing and maintaining any type of garden in the Rocky Mountains requires considerations unique to the area.

This broad region includes Santa Fe and Taos, the Front Range from Denver to Fort Collins, the Wasatch Mountains from Provo to Salt Lake City and Ogden, southern Wyoming, western Montana, and Idaho. Ecozones stretch from the Great Plains grasslands transition to pinyon-juniper foothills, the vast sagebrush steppe surrounding the mountain flanks, pine-Douglas-fir montane forests, spruce-fir subalpine forests, and alpine zones. Major cities and urban areas vary in altitude from 4,000 feet to 10,000 feet with snowfall and total annual precipitation varying from 8 to 50 inches annually. So saying one size does not fit all is an understatement. When considering plants for your habitat garden, pay close attention to the USDA cold hardiness zones and the plant's native habitats mentioned in the descriptions.

The major population areas in the Rockies encompass about six USDA ecoregion provinces. Each province is defined by different heat, rain, and temperature profiles and the plant communities they support. The region's USDA cold hardiness zones range from 4a with lows of -30° F, to 7b with lows of a +10° F. Rocky Mountain gardens commonly experience extended droughts with variations of 30° F. in a single day. Climate models promise a near future with hotter, drier conditions that will stress even the most adaptable native flora and fauna.

Which is all the more reason to create a pollinator haven in your yard.

LIFE ZONES

With a 3,000-mile (4,828 km) north–south latitudinal change and elevations varying from 1,000 to 14,000 feet (305–4,268 m), the Rocky Mountains encompass a mosaic of vegetation zones from semi-desert to alpine tundra. For every 1,000-foot (305 m) gain in elevation up a mountain slope, the temperature drops 3 degrees Fahrenheit (1.7 °C), and precipitation increases about 4 inches (10 cm).

The vegetation community of any one area depends on a number of factors, including elevation; average annual precipitation and temperature; number of growing days; soil type and depth; and even the frequency of rains, floods, winds, and fires. At any single location, the abiotic factors with the greatest influence are moisture and temperature, both influenced significantly by the aspect—the angle of the sun's solar radiation that warms the plants and dries the soil. Classically, south-facing slopes are hotter and drier, while north-facing slopes are wetter and cooler, each with dramatically different plant life.

The vegetation of the Rockies can be divided into major life zones. Some plants have special adaptations that match only a narrow niche within a single life zone (alpine plants, wetland orchids). Many are more generalist and common throughout two or more life zones. In most instances, life zones create vegetation mosaics that gradually transition from one to another, like junipers slowly encroaching on grasslands as foothills gain elevation. Others, like the treeline separating subalpine forests from alpine, can be dramatic and easy to detect.

Being able to recognize these life zones—and where your native plant garden fits in—is important, as it ensures a good match between the species you're planting and the likely conditions they'll face. **Note:** Every species mentioned in the summary below is included in the book—as not all of them (e.g., large trees) are typically thought of as garden plants; however, it's helpful to know them and their place in the wider environment.

Grasslands

Mixed-grass and short-grass prairies of the Great Plains parallel the eastern front of the Rockies for 3,000 miles (4,828 km) from New Mexico through Colorado, Wyoming, and Montana. The high plateau, semi-arid grasslands dominate between 5,000–7,000 feet (1,524–2,133 m), often reaching into the pinyon-juniper/mountain mahogany foothills along valleys, rolling hills, riparian woods, and dry slopes.

Grasslands integrate with sage species in the sagebrush steppe ecosystem, and they are prominent components in the intermountain parks, plateaus, and basins. Semi-arid, sun-loving wildflowers, such as buckwheats, and sunflowers thrive in this zone.

Sagebrush Steppe

Vast expanses of sagebrush dominate the plateaus and basins of the Intermountain West, primarily west of the Continental Divide, except in the Wyoming Basin where it spreads east into the Great Plains grasslands.

It occurs between 5,000–over 10,000 feet (1,525–over 3,048 m) on moderately deep, coarse soils. Big sagebrush *(Artemisia tridentata)* and other *Artemisia* species create a shrub-dominated overstory with an understory of perennial grasses and wildflowers. Other widespread shrubs include antelope bitterbush and rabbitbrush, with buckwheats and lupines among the most common wildflowers.

Foothills

As the transition zone between low-elevation grasslands and mid-elevation montane forests, the semi-arid woodlands and shrub communities occur on the lower slopes and foothills of mountain ranges. In the Southern Rockies, an association of pinyon pine, juniper, scrub oak, and mountain mahogany dominates the slopes from about 5,500–8,000 feet (1,676–2,438 m). Gambel's oak, spreading by roots, can form dense stands on sunny slopes, especially in fire scars.

As a transition community, the composition of the Foothills zone varies greatly from south to north. In the Middle Rockies, mountain mahogany, antelope bitterbush, and rabbitbrush become the dominant species.

Montane Forests

Mid-elevation forests stretch between the shrubby foothills and the spruce-fir subalpine forests. Ranging from 7,500–9,500 feet (2,286–2,895 m) in the Southern Rockies, ponderosa pine dominates east of the Continental Divide and Douglas-fir to the west. In the Middle Rockies, ponderosa pine mingles with Douglas-fir, and lodgepole pine forms dense stands. In moist forests west of the Continental Divide that receive Pacific maritime moisture, western red cedar, western hemlock, and grand fir dominate between 2,000–5,000 feet (6,190–1,524 m).

Subalpine Forests

These conifer forests occur between the upper montane forests and treeline. Dense forests are intermingled with wet and dry meadows, rolling grasslands, and open avalanche chutes. Engelmann spruce and subalpine fir dominate, along with stands of lodgepole pine and aspen. The spruce-fir belt extends 9,500–11,500 feet (2,895–3,350 m) in the Southern Rockies, 2,900–6,500 feet (884–1,980 m) in the Middle and Northern Rockies west of the Continental Divide, and 5,200–8,800 feet (1,585–2,682 m) east of the Divide. On high-elevation, dry, exposed slopes, stands of lodgepole and whitebark pine often dominate.

Alpine

Above treeline, cold temperatures make the growing season too short for trees to survive. Going south, the elevation of treeline increases steadily at the rate of 330 feet (100 m) per degree of latitude. Trees near their physiological limits become stunted or dwarfed. Despite the harsh environment of the alpine tundra, wildflowers abound. Fed by snowmelt, the tundra bursts with color as flowers race to bloom and set seed during the short July–August growing season.

Before You Plant: Create a Master Plan

All too often, gardeners see a pretty plant in a nursery and make a spur-of-the-moment purchase, then plant it in a spot that gives it little chance to survive, much less thrive. The goal here is to plan ahead to create a verdant, low-maintenance garden oasis with maximum pollinator benefit and prolonged seasonal beauty while minimizing expenses from plant loss, replacement, and water usage.

Analyze Your Yard The first thing a professional landscaper would do for you is draw a plot of your yard to scale (e.g., 1 inch equals 5 or 10 feet), so that's the best way for homeowners to start as well. Nothing fancy—just sketch in existing plants, walkways, walls, and fences. Then get creative. First, consider where you want individual specimen and accent plants; then fill in more-extensive border, entry, patio, and window-view gardens; and, if you have room, include landscape ovals and islands and mass plantings. Decide where you need low-growing foreground and border flowers; medium-size midgarden plants; and taller background shrubs and trees. Noting the mature sizes in the plant profiles, leave room for the plants to fill out.

Observe Sun Exposure The amount of sun and water a plant receives are perhaps the most critical factors for a plant's survival. Most vegetation in the lower elevation grassland-sage shrub steppe and foothill pinyon-juniper-oak woodlands receives full, direct sun, broken only with filtered shade from nearby small-leafed shrubs Even in the mixed-conifer montane and subalpine forests, plants thrive in meadows, open slopes, and forest edges with full-to-part sun daily.

Most native plants that thrive in the metropolitan areas require full sun to dappled shade. In the Plant Profiles, **Full Sun** means exposure to direct sun for 6 or more hours a day. **Partial Shade** is 4–5 hours of no sun. Sun-adapted plants compromised by too much shade respond with reduced blooming and leggy growth, or they die.

Now look at the shadow footprint of your house, walls, trees, and other shade-producing structures. From the shady north side of your house to the broiling southwest side, each nook and cranny creates a microhabitat guaranteed to affect how well a plant performs. Besides limiting sun exposure, a shady winter exposure can reduce the ground temperature in the root zone of a perennial by 10 degrees below the area's average low. Conversely, the reflected summer heat from a masonry wall can easily raise a plant's sustained heat load by 10 or more degrees.

Soil: Minerals, Nutrients & Air

Soil types vary across the region, and by elevation.

Plants need about 16 essential elements to grow, flower, and produce seeds. The carbon, oxygen, and hydrogen that produce carbohydrates required for plant growth come from air and water. Nitrogen (N), phosphorous (P), and potassium (K), the three compounds in chemical fertilizers, come from minerals and micro-organisms in the soil. The availability of roots to absorb these major and secondary compounds, and other micronutrients, depends on the pH (acidity level) of the soil.

The mineral components of mountain soils tend to be coarse, fast draining, predominately derived from limestone, and with a pH between 7 (neutral) and 8.5 (slightly alkaline). Soils derived from decomposed granite, especially in foothills areas below granite mountains, tend to be slightly acidic. Native plants are perfectly adapted to thrive in the variations of native soil textures and pH, so only minor soil amendment may be required. However, introduced plants adapted to more-acid soils (pH 6–7) may struggle to absorb the minerals and nutrients they need, especially phosphorous, iron, and zinc.

Phosphorous is necessary for plant growth, photosynthesis, and sugar production. Deficiencies in nitrogen, phosphorous, or iron cause chlorosis (leaves with yellowish areas between the green veins). Zinc deficiency causes malformed and damaged leaves. Avoid interplanting natives with exotics that require more acidic soils, or that have a higher water demand.

The native plants in your garden usually will not need strong doses of fertilizer or soil amendments to adjust the pH. A little compost worked into the soil surface and a thin layer of organic mulch to help retain soil moisture are usually all that is needed. Use a pH soil test kit, available from garden centers, if you have reason to think a serious imbalance may exist.

PRECIOUS WATER, POOR SOILS

The dominant soils in the Rocky Mountain region are fast-draining, sandy, gravelly; loamy in the foothills, shortgrass prairie, and sage shrub zones; with well-draining, humus-rich soils high in organics in the forested zones. Productive native soils in most low- to mid-elevation metropolitan and urban areas contain about 50% air and 50% minerals (sand, silt, clay). Organics in the surface layer (composted plant material, microorganisms, fungi, bacteria) comprise only about 1% of the total. The soil gaps provide oxygen necessary for the roots to respire. The spaces fill with water, the roots absorb nutrients and minerals, then the water drains and the roots breathe again. The roots completely dry out between rains. That's the water-and-soil formula for successful native plant gardens and landscapes.

The Rockies are famous for their vibrant wildflower displays in spring and summer.

Rocky Mountain native plants and their bloom cycles vary dramatically from the grasslands and foothills at 4,000 feet elevation to the alpine tundra above treeline. By June, spring has come and gone in the surrounding plains and foothills and summer temperatures are rising, while spring and snowmelt are just arriving in the subalpine forests above 9,500 feet. High-altitude afternoon thunderstorms are common. The plains, plateaus, high desert valleys, and foothills receive as little as 8–15 inches annual precipitation, the montane forest zone gets 20–40 inches, and the subalpine and alpine zones receive 40–60 inches total precipitation annually. Rocky Mountain home landscapes vary from xeriscape to lush and meadow-like.

Too little water limits blooming and growth, and it makes plants look rangy and unappealing in a garden setting. Too much water can cause root rot, and garden soil rich in humus and organics can smother roots adapted to coarse soils with a high oxygen content. Fortunately, native plants are adaptable, so establishing a good water balance and maintaining a verdant garden isn't too difficult to manage if you stay with plants adapted to your surroundings.

The best way to extend blooming through periods of summer drought dormancy and maintain a lush, vibrant garden that keeps pollinators coming back is with a regulated drip irrigation system. Soaker hoses looped along a border or through a garden, drip emitters at the base of individual plants, and mini-spray emitters for pocket gardens will saturate the soil surface on a regular schedule set by a timer. Vary the daily duration and how many days a week according to the garden's seasonal needs.

One heavy thunderstorm can produce hundreds of gallons of water that cascades off the average roof. If you don't catch the overflow in cisterns for future watering needs, it soaks into the ground and builds up a soil moisture bank. Most urban yards are sloped away from the house so that the water slowly percolates through the soil downslope, creating a simulated seep-spring effect. Or you can incorporate a sculpted landscaped drainage into your master design so that water is not lost to runoff into the street. Depending on your base soil type, captured roof runoff could easily supply enough moisture to sustain a large tree or several shrubs, or an oval garden packed with wildflowers.

Gardening from the Ground Up

All too often, developers and their landscape architects create cookie-cutter subdivisions lined with yards covered with turf grass and one shrub or tree. A pollinator garden can transform a yard from a sterile layer of high-maintenance, thirsty turf grass into an organic, three-dimensional landscape.

A living landscape starts from the ground up, or specifically the fungus, bacteria, and microbes several inches below the surface. Bees dig nest burrows in bare ground, beetle and moth larvae pupate just below the surface, worms and bugs decompose organic matter in the upper soil layers, and ground-foraging birds scratch for tidbits in the leaf litter.

Weed or Wildflower?

It depends on your perspective. Many cities and homeowners' associations wage a vicious battle against vagrant wildflowers, as well as the noxious invasives. "All weeds!" they declare and arm the troops with herbicides. Yet to pollinators, wildflowers are rich sources of pollen and nectar, as well as larval host plants. To a bee, the sterile petunias, pansies, hybrids, and cultivars with no pollen or nectar that fill many gardens are the invasive weeds.

Rocky Mountain gardens are not as overrun with unwanted intruders as gardens in wetter, warmer climates, but some weed control is inevitably needed. Manual removal is usually the most efficient, and far preferable to spraying a broad-spectrum herbicide with glyphosate (Roundup). Court cases with billion-dollar settlements have ruled glyphosate a carcinogen, and many counties and municipalities in the West have banned its use on public property. If spraying is required, a popular effective solution is easy to make. To one gallon of white vinegar, mix 2 cups Epsom salt and ¼ cup liquid dish soap. Apply with a pump-type sprayer. The spray kills the foliage and shallow roots, but not necessarily deep taproots unless you stream it on the base of the plant to soak in.

An invasive species, the ox-eye daisy is now found in much of the region.

Mulching is one of the most important ways to manage weeds and sustain a healthy, living soil. The two general types of mulch, organic and inorganic, have a place in pollinator gardens. A modest layer of shredded bark, leaves, or compost around plants will keep the root zone cooler, slow soil evaporation, decrease water usage, add nutrients, and inhibit weed growth. A light layer of shredded bark will stabilize loose sandy areas without inhibiting bee and larvae nesting.

Accent boulders and smaller rocks along borders and in pattern designs play dual roles as attractive design elements and important micro-habitat stabilizers. The soil under a rock is cooler, retains moisture from condensation, and harbors a community of invertebrates relished by thrashers, towhees, and lizards.

One last consideration with your master plan is how formal you want your pollinator garden and yard landscape. Neat and tidy, or more toward the wildscape look? Do you want a magazine-cover garden and yard with trimmed shrubs and confined borders, or a naturalized habitat with a leaf-and-limb pile in the corner and a "forest" of 5-foot-tall sunflowers against the back wall? Whether you have room only for a few container plants on your balcony, a small landscape island, or a full-scale garden design for your yard, the butterflies, bees, and birds will benefit, and you will help repair the habitat lost by our housing developments.

ABCs for a Pollinator Habitat Garden

The Xerces Society, National Wildlife Society, native plant societies, and national and state agencies and organizations have certification programs for creating backyard wildlife habitats. They vary in particulars, but all center around certain basics: Supply year-round sources of food, water, shelter, and nesting sites; plant at least 50% native plants; use no herbicides or pesticides; and avoid nursery plants treated with systemic neonicotinoids, which produce pollen and nectar poisonous to bees.

Gardens that cater specifically to pollinators have a few additional design requirements.

Water The first key element in your backyard oasis is a dependable source of water. Birds are attracted to the traditional bird bath, or you can get fancier with a solar-powered fountain, such as one with water cascading through different-sized bowls. Bees like still, shallow water—a pan with pebbles on a drip emitter works great. Butterflies need moist soil, so an emitter on the ground, a garden with a drip system mini-spray, or bird bath overflow is all they need.

Food Pollinators need energy-rich nectar and protein-rich pollen from the time they first emerge in the early spring, while foraging and nesting through the summer, and in the fall until they migrate or overwinter. Diversity is the rule in selecting plants, both to maintain a three-seasonal bloom, and to present a variety of sizes and shapes to attract a diversity of butterflies, bees, other insect pollinators, and hummingbirds. Avoid nursery hybrids and selections that produce flamboyant flowers but little pollen and nectar. A sugar-water feeder for hummingbirds will help supplement the natural flower food sources.

Shelter All animals need a refuge from wind, rain, and midday heat, and protection from predators. Butterflies need a sunny place to bask and warm up in the morning, and birds need shady day perches to rest while foraging, and leafy, protected night perches. A mix of perennial wildflowers, shrubs, a small tree, and several clumps of bunch grasses will provide the necessary shelter.

Nest Sites A diverse population of pollinators cannot be sustainable without successful nesting. For butterflies and moths, this means larval host plants. Each species lays its eggs on only the specific native plants that will nourish its caterpillars. Pretty exotic plants may supply lots of nectar and pollen, but only native plants will host the caterpillars. Most native bees are solitary and lay their eggs, along with a pollen ball for the larvae to eat, in a ground burrow they excavate, or a cavity they find or drill in stems or limbs. Burrowing bees need bare ground free of thick mulch or other dense covering. Bee hotels with a variety of sized holes and tubes are popular for hole-nesting bees. Bunch grasses harbor overwintering bees and moth larvae.

Selecting Plants

Diversity is the key. Gardens with a variety of flower sizes and shapes attract the most kinds and numbers of pollinators. A well-balanced garden has a mix of annual and long-blooming perennial flowers and a few early-blooming shrubs. Leafy shrubs and a small- to medium-size tree will provide shelter from sun and wind and nesting sites for birds and bees. Also include at least two species of bunch grass for moth larvae and overwintering bees.

Blanket flower is a popular native plant.

You can usually look at a plant and tell what pollinates it. Some plants use a generalist strategy that offers a rich nectar-pollen buffet to all comers. These are garden favorites because of the large numbers and kinds of pollinators they attract. Members of the aster, rose, and verbena families include generalist plants that attract a variety of insects.

Conversely, many plants conserve resources by catering to a select few pollinators. No garden is complete without a selection of specialty flowers that add rich colors and attract iconic pollinators. Salvias, penstemons, and datura all attract unique pollinators. The special characteristics that adapt a flower to a particular class of pollinators are called **syndromes.** Syndromes are only general rules of thumb since insects will often go wherever the food is available.

PLANTING USING PLANT SYNDROMES

Bee Syndrome Flowers are typically shades of yellows and blues with nectar guides; tubular with an inflated shape to fit specifically sized bees, or open and bowl-shaped for all bees; petals form a landing pad; nectar glands secrete abundant nectar and stamens produce rich pollen; flowers are faintly scented. Members of the aster, verbena, and legume families include many plants attractive to bees.

Butterfly Syndrome Flowers are bright reds and purples with nectar guides; tubular shaped with a narrow throat; petals offer a wide landing pad; produce more nectar than pollen since butterflies don't gather pollen; faintly scented. Almost every native plant hosts some types of caterpillars, but milkweeds are necessary for monarchs and queens, and they provide abundant nectar for many insects.

Moth Syndrome Flowers are white or light colors visible in moonlight; large and showy or small but in conspicuous clusters; narrow, tubular throat; nocturnal or crepuscular bloom times; strongly scented; flowers last one day. Members of the evening primrose and four-o'clock families are ideal for nocturnal gardens.

Beetle Syndrome Flowers are white or greenish, dish-shaped, produce abundant pollen and nectar, and strongly scented. Beetles, some of nature's most colorful and diverse pollinators, have been pollinating flowers for 150 million years and feast on the pollen, petals, and developing seeds of almost any flower.

Hummingbird Syndrome Flowers are bright red to orange, tubular shaped to fit bird bills; have no landing pad, guidelines, or scent; and produce abundant nectar. Penstemons, honeysuckles, and salvias add brilliant color and attract hummingbirds, but the birds will sip from almost any flower. Maintain a sugar-water feeder (¼ cup sugar to 1 cup water) as a dependable source of food.

Native plants, such as this penstemon, are hummingbird magnets.

The Basics of Plant Anatomy

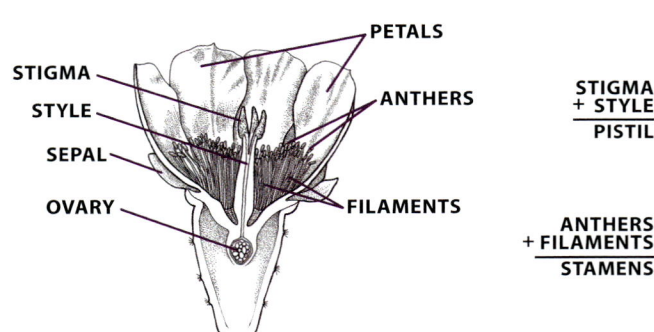

PARTS OF A FLOWER

Flower anatomy has diverged radically among plant species to attract a diversity of pollinators with the twin rewards of protein-rich pollen and energy-rich nectar. From thorny cacti to flamboyant lupines, sunflowers, and penstemons, the various parts of a plant are basically the same. Yet plants have modified and perfected every anatomical feature to not only attract pollinators but also survive in the most hostile of environments.

Flowers serve one obvious purpose: to produce seeds for the continued survival of the plant. Many trees, grasses, and weedy plants eschew dependence on animal pollinators and produce nondescript flowers that scatter copious amounts of pollen to the winds. The windborne misery of hay fever victims creates a booming industry for allergy doctors and medication. Conversely, the beauty of a colorful flower inspires poetry, romance, and a wonder for the majesty of nature.

FLOWERS

The taxonomy of a flower defines the plant's species, groups it in a genus of similar plants, and assigns it to a family with broadly related features. The flower itself is a collection of modified leaves. Leaflike bracts grow on the stem beneath the flower. They are typically green, but some flowers, like paintbrushes, have bracts that are showier than the petals. **Sepals** surround and protect the bud and clasp the bottom of the flower. **Petals** are usually the showy feature and are colored and marked to attract specific pollinators. They may spread open widely or be united to form a narrow tube that opens with lobes. **Stamens,** the male feature, are thin filaments topped with pollen-covered **anthers.** The **pistil,** the female feature, consists of a tubular style, containing the ovaries, topped with a **stigma** with lobes that receive the pollen. The shape of the stamen and stigma are often highly specialized to fit certain pollinators.

FLOWER CLUSTERS

To increase pollination efficiency, flowers make gathering pollen and nectar as efficient as possible for the pollinator. Flying from flower to flower takes considerable energy, so plants with single flowers on a stem, especially annuals, are often synchronized to bloom all at the same time. Flower clusters offer dozens of small flowers together so pollinators don't have to waste energy searching. Round or flat clusters provide a compact source of nectar and pollen, while spikes of flowers usually start blooming at the bottom so flowers bloom over an extended time. Lupine and milkvetch flowers often have white banner petals that turn red when pollinated so bees won't waste energy on flowers with no more nectar. Penstemon flowers are often on one side of the spike so hummingbirds and bumblebees can simply move upward and not have to circle the stem. Members of the aster family have composite flower heads: showy, petal-like ray flowers surround a compact disk with dozens of small, tubular disk-shaped florets that produce pollen and nectar for a wide variety of pollinators.

Round-to-flat cluster

Spike

Composite

LEAVES

The shape, size, and color of leaves, the food factories of a plant, can offer an extra ornamental dimension to a landscape. The size of a leaf can vary from a fraction of an inch (blue paloverde) to several feet long (fern and palm fronds). The shape can range from a simple oval or a deeply dissected or lobed blade to a compound leaf with dozens of tiny leaflets. To reduce water loss by transpiration, leaves and leaflets in deserts tend to be small, often with waxy or densely woolly surfaces, and may be deciduous in summer. Sun-loving plants die in the shade because sun- and shade-adapted plants produce carbohydrates using different photosynthetic pathways.

Leaves, as well as flowers, are an important feature in identifying a plant. Some flowers have a dense rosette of basal leaves, especially biennials that germinate the first year and overwinter as a rosette, then bloom the second year. Notice if the leaves grow opposite or alternate each other, or in whorls around the stem. Does the leaf clasp the stem or have a short stalk (petiole)? Are the blades simple or compound? Are the margins (edges) wavy, lobed, or smooth? Are the surfaces hairy, rough, or smooth? Leaf features all help a plant adapt to its environment.

Urban Wildlife

With the continuing loss of wildlife habitat to urban sprawl, several small mammals species now take refuge in parks, open space preserves, greenbelts, and even vacant lots. Coyotes, foxes, feral and domestic cats, rabbits, raccoons, skunks, and other small mammals from time to time may visit pollinator gardens and backyard wildscapes. Some, like deer, rabbits, and chipmunks, that feast on tender garden plants, may become nuisances and need to be fenced out, or delectable plants may be caged in. The Species Profiles indicate which plants are deer and rabbit resistant.

Any garden, especially one designed to be insect-friendly, will attract its share of creepy-crawly visitors. You might expect to see ants, spiders, scorpions, and centipedes. Black widow spiders with their shiny black bodies with red ventral spots, are one critter to look out for. They favor dark corners like tool sheds, woodpiles, and even underneath patio chairs and tables. Unlike orb spiders, they build chaotic, tangled webs. Bites cause varying amounts of pain and discomfort, but over-the-counter pain medication usually suffices. Simple precautions like wearing gardening gloves when cleaning up or working in your garden usually provides ample protection. Most of these critters are delectable tidbits for ground-foraging birds and seldom a problem.

Embracing Our Biological Heritage

Plants and pollinators are a part of our great natural heritage. Why can't our neighborhoods represent the natural plant diversity that existed before our houses were built? Our children could grow up familiar with the same plants that provided food and fiber for the Indigenous Peoples who have lived in the Mountain West for thousands of years. The plants that have sunk their roots in Rocky Mountain soil since the last Ice Age can help us understand that our psyches and society are equally rooted to the earth. As our pollinator gardens flower and fruit, we will be rewarded by the sight of butterflies dancing from flower to flower and by the melodies of birds singing in our trees.

Meet the Pollinators

Fossil records of beetles and flowers indicate that the pollination saga began about 150 million years ago. Since then, bees, butterflies, moths, flies, and wasps have joined the diverse cast, but the flowers themselves have always retained ultimate control of the show. The floral masters of manipulation have devised ways beyond the limits of human imagination to direct pollinator behavior. Using rewards (energy-rich nectar and protein-rich pollen), deception, false advertising, bait and switch, entrapment, and even lethal measures, flowers engineer insects to transport their pollen in the most energy-efficient ways. This eons-old drama continues today on every flower in your pollinator garden.

BEES

The Rockies is paradise for bees. Of the more than 4,000 species that live in North America, at least 1,500 call our shrublands, plains, foothills, and mountains home. These rock stars of the pollination world are the only animals that deliberately collect pollen. Adult bees feed on nectar and, with special hairs designed to hold pollen grains, the females collect pollen to store in their brood chambers for larvae to eat. Most bees are generalist feeders, but some prefer specific family, genera, or even a single species of flowering plants. Though some bumblebees are social, 90% of bees are solitary with each female creating her own set of brood chambers. She digs a burrow in bare ground, tunnels into a plant stem, or uses a preexisting cavity. In a garden setting, easily constructed "bee hotels" with a variety of hole sizes drilled in wood often fill up quickly.

At the end of her life, at approximately 6 weeks, the female seals off the last chamber and dies. The larvae develop over the winter and emerge in the spring just in time for the early-blooming flowers. By some unknown clues, specialty feeders synchronize their emergence with the bloom of their preferred species. Some may extend their dormancy several years if droughts suppress blooming.

Bees in the Rockies vary in size from smaller than a grain of rice to robust, 1-inch-long bumblebees. Large bees can forage over a mile in distance, medium-size bees range over 400–500 yards, small bees venture 200 yards, and tiny bees can be confined to 200 feet. Ideally, the population of bees in your garden will be able to find the food and nesting sites in your and your neighbors' backyard gardens to complete their entire life cycle.

1. Valley carpenter bee (*Xylocopa sonorina*) **2.** Western honeybee (*Apis mellifera*) **3.** Cactus bee (*Lithurgopsis* spp.) **4.** Metallic green bee (*Agapostemon melliventris*) **5.** Megachile bee (*Megachile* spp.) **6.** Hunt's bumblebee (*Bombus huntii*)

BUTTERFLIES

Of the approximately 800 species of butterflies in North America, about 200 occur in the Rockies. With brilliant colors and intricate patterns, these charismatic insects are one of the star attractions in a pollinator garden. Ironically, in the scheme of efficient pollination, butterflies fall near the bottom of the list. With long legs that often hold them above the flower's pollen-bearing anthers, a long tongue to probe deep into the flower, and no body hair designed to collect pollen, butterflies pollinate by accident, not by design. Even so, they are critically important to the health and stability of the ecosystem's complex food chain.

During their adult lifespan of 1–2 weeks, the females lay hundreds of eggs on specific host plants. The eggs hatch into caterpillars that relentlessly devour plant foliage. They increase their body mass by 10,000 times before entering metamorphosis. These juicy tidbits of protein feed the world of the wild. Ninety-five percent of songbirds depend on caterpillar protein to rear their hatchlings.

In the winter, or in times of drought, butterflies go into **diapause,** a period of suspended growth similar to hibernation. Diapause can occur in any life stage: eggs, larvae, chrysalis, or adults. A butterfly may be several years old by the time it becomes an adult. During winter diapause, caterpillars (of both butterflies and moths) nest in fallen leaves, tree bark, bunch grass stubble, or underground; chrysalides hang on protected twigs; and adults hide in woodpiles, cracks, or under loose bark. So when you tidy up your garden in the winter, be sure to reserve a place for overwintering butterflies and moths.

In the Rockies, butterfly activity peaks July through September, depending on elevation. Darting from flower to flower or dancing in the sunlight overhead, they delight all ages. My preschool daughter called them "flutterbys," which I think best describes these amazing creatures.

1. Arizona sister (*Adelpha eulalia*) **2.** Gulf fritillary (*Agraulis vanillae*) **3.** Monarch (*Danaus plexippus*) **4.** Two-tailed swallowtail (*Papilio multicaudata*) **5.** Black swallowtail (*Papilio polyxenes*) **6.** Painted lady (*Vanessa cardui*)

MOTHS

As night falls, nature's night shift takes over. In a pollinator garden, that means moths, one of the most numerous and efficient classes of pollinators. With 12,000 species in the United States and 1,000 in the Rockies, moth species outnumber butterflies 12 to 1. Note the antennae: male moths have feathery, comb-like antennae, while the females' are smooth and pointed; butterflies have smooth antennae with a swollen, club-like tip. Moths vary in size from ¼ inch to hummingbird-sized sphinx and hawkmoths. They can be diurnal (police car moths), but most are crepuscular (sphinx and hawkmoths) or nocturnal.

Moths have the same metamorphic life cycle and host plant requirements as butterflies, but more are plant specialists. Many plants have long floral tubes pollinated only by long-tongued moths, while some emit puffs of sweet aroma into the night to attract moths from far distances. Sacred datura produces a high-octane, sugar-rich nectar laced with addictive hallucinogens to keep the sphinx moths coming back night after night. As another example, each species of yucca depends on a single species of moth for pollination. The moth gathers pollen from one yucca and deposits it in the specially shaped stigma of a nearby yucca, then lays her eggs in the ovary so the larvae can eat the developing seeds. The larvae pupate in the ground and mysteriously don't emerge until the yucca flowers again, which may take years.

Moths aren't as showy as butterflies, but they are a vital part of the ecosystem food chain. Ninety-five percent of songbirds feed their nestlings moth caterpillars found on tree and shrub leaves, and many ground-foraging birds feast on the nearly 50% of moths that pupate in leaf litter, bunch grass thatch, and shallow soil. So be sure to include a selection of night-blooming wildflowers in your garden, such as the evening primrose (Onagraceae) and four-o'clock (Nyctaginaceae) families.

1. White-lined sphinx moth (*Hyles lineata*) **2.** Police car moth (*Gnophaela vermiculata*) **3.** Columbia silk moth (*Hyalophora columbia*) **4.** Rustic sphinx moth (*Manduca rustica*) **5.** Army cutworm moth (*Euxoa auxiliaris*) **6.** Tiger moth (*Pyrrharctia isabella*)

FLIES

Don't gasp at the thought of attracting flies to your pollinator garden. This diverse order, with 125,000 classified species worldwide, includes many pollinators that are second in importance only to bees. Flies have been recorded visiting at least 71 plant families. At higher altitudes with cool mornings and during inclement weather, flies are active much longer during the day than bees. Flies vary in size from mere specks to an inch long. Many native flies are hairy and easily confused for bees, but flies have nubby antennae and big eyes while bees have long antennae and smaller eyes.

Flies, especially hover flies (Syrphid family), are an important component of a pollinator habitat. The adults feed on nectar as they pollinate, and the larvae help control insect damage to plants. As carnivorous predators, the larvae complete the food web by feeding on aphids, spiders, other insects, and detritus. Most flies have short tongues and feed on shallow, flat flowers. They are critical pollinators for many plants in the carrot/parsley family (Apiaceae), aster family (Asteraceae), many annuals and small-flowering shade plants, and more than 100 human food plants (chocolate, carrots, tree fruits, berries, avocados, mangos).

1. Bee fly (*Hemipenthes* spp.) **2.** Grasshopper bee fly (*Systoechus vulgaris*) **3.** Flower fly (*Syrphus* spp.) **4.** Red tachinid fly (*Adejeania vexatrix*) **5.** Beelike tachinid fly (*Hystricia abrupta*) **6.** Tachinid fly (Tachinidae genera)

BEETLES

Though thought to be the first insects to start the complex coevolution relationship between insects and flowers 150 million years ago, today beetles are minor players in the saga. Yet with 30,000 species in the United States, and 340,000 and counting in the world, the impact of beetles on the plant world is immense. Though much of their activity is detrimental, such as the conifer forest devastation by bark beetles, they play critical roles as pollinators, decomposers, and predators, such as lady bugs that eat aphids both as larvae and adults. Beetles are necessary and beneficial in a well-balanced habitat and generally welcomed inhabitants in our gardens. Several beetle families are important pollinators, but more by their clumsy rambling over flowers as they gulp nectar; munch away on pollen, petals, and flower parts; and search for sex partners. Scores of small beetles congregate in a single cactus flower, dozens of soldier beetles crawl over the dense flower heads of goldenrods, while a single red-and-black flower beetle poses like a king of a flower. Beetles are some of the most bizarre and flamboyantly colored insects you'll find in nature and thrilling visitors in your garden.

1. Fire-colored beetle (*Pyrochroa* spp.) **2.** Goldenrod soldier beetle (*Chauliognathus pennsylvanicus*) **3.** Longhorn beetle (*Crossidius humeralis*) **4.** Red longhorn beetle (*Crossidius militaris*) **5.** Spotted Tylosis longhorn beetle (*Tylosis maculatus*) **6.** Soldier beetle (*Chauliognathus* spp.)

BIRDS

According to the National Audubon Society, Americans spend more money on birdfeed and binoculars than on hunting and ammunition. By supplying the habitat needs of birds, your back window or patio can be an exciting place to bird-watch. A yard oasis with shrubs and trees for nesting and shelter, fruit- and seed-bearing plants and a seed feeder for dependable food, and a constant water source will support year-round resident birds and attract seasonal migrants.

Only one hummingbird, the ruby-throated, is common east of the Mississippi River, while six species nest or regularly migrate or visit into much of the Rockies. Stock your garden with hummingbird-adapted plants with tubular red flowers, such as penstemons and mints, supplemented with a sugar-water feeder to ensure a constant food source, and your garden will be a magnet for these energetic jewels of the bird world.

How to Use This Book

The native plants in this book are organized by type, with sections for **Trees, Shrubs, Wildflowers, Vines & Groundcovers,** and **Grasses.** Each plant profile includes key information about the plant's size and growth pattern, hardiness zone, bloom period, companion plants, and what it attracts, as well as a more detailed description of the plant.

You can either find plants that strike your fancy by paging through the profiles in the body of the book, or you can consult the information in the back. See page 260 for a list of plants that attract butterflies, page 262 for plants that attract bees, page 266 for plants that attract feeding and nesting birds, and page 267 for plants that specifically attract hummingbirds. Page 264 lists plants that are good for container gardening. Page 268 has a list of butterflies/moths with host plants for their caterpillars.

For information and inspiration, visit one of the botanical gardens listed on page 273 to see and compare mature native plants in landscape settings; then you can draw a plot of your garden and sketch in prospective plants. Turn to page 271 for a list of native plant retail suppliers in Colorado, New Mexico, and Wyoming. Finally, check page 272 for a list of **Rocky Mountain Native Plant Society** chapters.

Rocky Mountain Plants at a Glance

To help organize your garden plant wish list, or to add new plants to existing plots, the following at-a-glance table helps you decide what and where to plant. It includes the hardiness zone; blooming period; whether a plant attracts butterflies, bees, or birds; and its likely deer/rabbit resistance.

For a well-balanced garden, choose a selection of plants that will provide blooms from early spring, through the summer, and into the fall until first frost. To maximize the numbers and diversity of pollinators, chose a mix of flowers with a variety of sizes and shapes. Remember, no plant is totally resistant to a hunger-stressed deer, chipmunk, or rabbit. If necessary, enclose young, tender plants in a wire cage.

Rocky Mountain Plants at a Glance

COMMON NAME	SCIENTIFIC NAME	ROCKY MOUNTAIN HARDINESS ZONES
TREES		
Colorado Blue Spruce pg. 41	*Picea pungens*	2a–8a
Gambel's Oak pg. 43	*Quercus gambelii*	4a–7b
Pinyon Pine pg. 45	*Pinus edulis*	5a–7b
Ponderosa Pine pg. 47	*Pinus ponderosa*	3a–7b
Quaking Aspen pg. 49	*Populus tremuloides*	1a–6b
Rocky Mountain Maple pg. 51	*Acer glabrum*	4a–8b
SHRUBS		
Alderleaf Mountain Mahogany, pg. 55	*Cercocarpus montanus*	5a–9b
Antelope Bitterbush pg. 57	*Purshia tridentata* var. *tridentata*	5b–10a
Blue Elderberry pg. 59	*Sambucus nigra* ssp. *cerulea*	6a–10b
Chokecherry pg. 61	*Prunus virginiana*	5a–10b
Ciffbush pg. 63	*Jamesia americana*	3a–8b
Cliff Fendlerbush pg. 65	*Fendlera rupicola*	4a–7b
Common Snowberry pg. 67	*Symphoricarpos albus* var. *laevigatus*	5a–9b
Fragrant Sumac pg. 69	*Rhus aromatica (tribolata)*	5a–10b
Golden Currant pg. 71	*Ribes aureum*	5a–10b; cold hardy to -38°F
Gooseberry Currant pg. 73	*Ribes montigenum*	4a–7a
Leadplant pg. 75	*Amorpha canescens*	4a–7b

ATTRACTS BUTTERFLIES	ATTRACTS BEES	ATTRACTS BIRDS	BLOOM PERIOD	DEER RESISTANT
host for moths	no	seeds, shelter	April–May	yes
host for moths	no	fruit, shelter, nesting	March–April	no
host	no	seeds, shelter, nesting	April–May	yes
host	no	seeds	April	yes
host	no	fruit, shelter	June	no
host	yes	fruit, shelter	April–May	yes
nectar, host	yes	no	May–June	no
nectar, host	yes	seeds, shelter	March–June	no
nectar, host	yes	seeds, shelter, nesting	May–August; fruit: August–October	yes
nectar, host	yes	fruit, shelter	May–June	yes
nectar, host	yes	shelter	May–June	yes
yes	yes	shelter	April–June	no
nectar, host	yes	fruit, shelter	May–July; fruit: fall–winter	yes
nectar, host	yes	seeds, shelter	March–May; fruit: July–October	yes
nectar, host	yes	fruit	April–June	yes
nectar, host	yes	fruit	June–August	yes
nectar, host	yes	no	May–July	yes

Rocky Mountain Plants at a Glance (continued)

	COMMON NAME	SCIENTIFIC NAME	ROCKY MOUNTAIN HARDINESS ZONES
	Lewis Mock Orange pg. 77	*Philadelphus lewisii*	4a–9b
	Mountain Ninebark pg. 79	*Physocarpus monogynus*	4a–8b
	Mountainspray pg. 81	*Holodiscus discolor (dumosus)*	5b–7b
	Red Elderberry pg. 83	*Sambucus racemosa*	3a–7b
	Red-osier Dogwood pg. 85	*Cornus sericea*	5a–10b
	Rubber Rabbitbrush pg. 87	*Ericameria nauseosa*	4a–9b
	Shrubby Cinquefoil pg. 89	*Dasiphora fruticosa*	3b–7b
	Smooth Sumac pg. 91	*Rhus glabra*	3a–9b
	Snakeweed, Broomweed pg. 93	*Gutierrezia sarothrae*	3a–10b
	Thimbleberry pg. 95	*Rubus parviflorus*	4a–6b
	Twinberry Honeysuckle pg. 97	*Lonicera involucrata*	5a–10b
	Western Mountain Ash pg. 99	*Sorbus sitchensis*	2a–7b
	Western Serviceberry pg. 101	*Amelanchier alnifolia*	4a–7b
	White Spirea pg. 103	*Spiraea betulifolia*	5a–8b
	Woods' Rose pg. 105	*Rosa woodsii*	4a–8a

WILDFLOWERS

	COMMON NAME	SCIENTIFIC NAME	ROCKY MOUNTAIN HARDINESS ZONES
	Black-eyed Susan pg. 109	*Rudbeckia hirta*	3a–7b
	Blanket Flower pg. 111	*Gaillardia aristata*	4a–7b
	Blue Flax pg. 113	*Linum lewisii*	4b–9b
	Butterfly Milkweed pg. 115	*Asclepias tuberosa*	3a–9b

ATTRACTS BUTTERFLIES	ATTRACTS BEES	ATTRACTS BIRDS	BLOOM PERIOD	DEER RESISTANT
nectar, host	yes	no	May–July	yes
yes	yes	fruit, shelter	May–July	yes
nectar, host	yes	shelter	May–August	yes
nectar, host	yes	fruit, shelter	March–July	moderately
nectar, host	yes	fruit, shelter	April–June	no
nectar, host	yes	shelter	July–October	yes
nectar, host	yes	no	June–September	yes
nectar, host	yes	fruit: winter, shelter	June–August; fruits may overwinter	yes
nectar, host	yes	no	July–November	yes
nectar, host	yes	fruit	May–August	yes
nectar, host	yes	fruit, shelter	June–July	yes
nectar, host	yes	fruit	March–June	no
nectar, host	yes	fruit, shelter	May–July	no
nectar, host	yes	no	May–July	yes
nectar, host	yes	no	April–August	yes
nectar, host	yes	no	June–September	yes
yes	yes	seeds	April–October (frost)	yes
nectar, host	yes	no	March–July	no
nectar, host	yes	hummingbirds	May–September	yes

Rocky Mountain Plants at a Glance (continued)

	COMMON NAME	SCIENTIFIC NAME	ROCKY MOUNTAIN HARDINESS ZONES
	Colorado Blue Columbine pg. 117	Aquilegia coerulea	3a–7b
	Colorado (Pinque) Rubberweed, pg. 119	Hymenoxys richardsonii	4a–7b
	Common Sunflower pg. 121	Helianthus annuus	2a–11a
	Common Yarrow pg. 123	Achillea millefolium	4a–9b
	Cutleaf Anemone pg. 125	Anemone multifida	3b–8b
	Desert Prince's Plume pg. 127	Stanleya pinnata	4a–9a
	Dwarf Larkspur pg. 129	Delphinium nuttallianum	6a–9a
	Fireweed pg. 131	Chamerion angustifolium	5a–10a
	Gayfeather pg. 133	Liatris punctata	4a–9b
	Golden Columbine pg. 135	Aquilegia chrysantha	3b–9b
	Golden Crownbeard pg. 137	Verbesina encelioides	5a–8b
	Greenthread pg. 139	Thelesperma filifolium	5a–9a
	Groundplum Milkvetch pg. 141	Astragalus crassicarpus	3b–6b
	Hairy False Goldenaster pg. 143	Heterotheca villosa	5a–8b
	Harebell pg. 145	Campanula rotundifolia	3a–6b
	Heartleaf Arnica pg. 147	Arnica cordifolia	5a–7b
	Hooked-spur Blue Violet pg. 149	Viola adunca	4a–9b
	Mountain Blue-eyed Grass pg. 151	Sisyrinchium montanum	4a–7b
	Mountain Golden Banner pg. 153	Thermopsis montana	4a–9b
	Narrowleaf Bluebells pg. 155	Mertensia lanceolata	4a–6b

ATTRACTS BUTTERFLIES	ATTRACTS BEES	ATTRACTS BIRDS	BLOOM PERIOD	DEER RESISTANT
yes	yes	hummingbirds	April–May	yes
yes	yes	no	May–September	yes
nectar, host	yes	seeds	June–August	yes
yes	yes	no	April–July	yes
moths	yes	no	March–July	yes
nectar, host	yes	no	April–September	yes
yes	yes	hummingbirds	March–July	yes
nectar, host	yes	hummingbirds	June–September	no
yes	yes	hummingbirds	August–October	yes
yes	yes	hummingbirds	April–September	no
nectar, host	yes	seeds	April–October	yes
yes	yes	no	May–September	yes
yes	yes	fruit, seeds	April–June	yes
yes	yes	no	June–September	yes
yes	yes	hummingbirds	June–October	yes
nectar, host	yes	no	May–July	no
nectar, host	yes	no	April–August	yes
yes	yes	no	April–July	yes
yes	yes	no	May–August	yes
nectar, host	yes	no	April–August	yes

Rocky Mountain Plants at a Glance (continued)

COMMON NAME	SCIENTIFIC NAME	ROCKY MOUNTAIN HARDINESS ZONES
Nettleleaf Giant Hyssop pg. 157	*Agastache urticifolia*	3a–9b
New Mexico Checkermallow pg. 159	*Sidalcea neomexicana*	4a–8b
Orange Sneezeweed pg. 161	*Hymenoxys hoopesii*	5b–7b
Pearly Everlasting pg. 163	*Anaphalis margaritacea*	3a–7b
Prairie Coneflower pg. 165	*Ratibida columnifera*	4a–9b
Prairie Spiderwort pg. 167	*Tradescantia occidentalis*	4a–9b
Purple Aster pg. 169	*Dieteria canescens*	4a–10b
Purple Locoweed pg. 171	*Oxytropis lambertii*	3a–8b
Purple Prairie-clover pg. 173	*Dalea purpurea*	4a–8b
Quamash pg. 175	*Camassia quamash*	4a–8b
Rocky Mountain Beeplant pg. 177	*Peritoma serrulata*	3a–8b
Rocky Mountain Groundsel pg. 179	*Packera streptanthifolia*	4a–7b
Rocky Mountain Iris pg. 181	*Iris missouriensis*	5a–7b
Rocky Mountain Penstemon pg. 183	*Penstemon strictus*	4a–9b
Rocky Mountain Phlox pg. 185	*Phlox multiflora*	3a–7b
Rydberg's Penstemon pg. 187	*Penstemon rydbergii*	4a–7b
Scarlet Globemallow pg. 189	*Sphaeralcea coccinea*	6a–8b
Showy Fleabane pg. 191	*Erigeron speciosus*	4a–7b
Showy Goldeneye pg. 193	*Heliomeris multiflora*	4a–8b
Showy Jacob's Ladder pg. 195	*Polemonium pulcherrimum*	5a–7b

ATTRACTS BUTTERFLIES	ATTRACTS BEES	ATTRACTS BIRDS	BLOOM PERIOD	DEER RESISTANT
yes	yes	hummingbirds	June–September	yes
nectar, host	yes	no	April–September	yes
yes	yes	no	July–August	yes
nectar, host	yes	no	June–September	yes
yes	yes	no	June–September	no
yes	yes	no	April–September	yes
nectar, host	yes	no	May–October	yes
nectar, host	yes	no	April–August	yes
nectar, host	yes	no	May–September	yes
yes	yes	no	April–May	yes
nectar, host	yes	yes	June–August	yes
nectar, host: moth	yes	no	May–September	yes
nectar, host	yes	hummingbirds	May–July	yes
nectar, host	yes	no	May–July	yes
yes	yes	no	June–August	yes
nectar, host	yes	hummingbirds	June–August	yes
nectar, host	yes	seeds	May–July	no
yes	yes	no	June–October	yes
yes	yes	no	July–October	yes
yes	yes	no	May–August	yes

Rocky Mountain Plants at a Glance (continued)

COMMON NAME	SCIENTIFIC NAME	ROCKY MOUNTAIN HARDINESS ZONES
Showy Milkweed pg. 197	*Asclepias speciosa*	3a–9b
Sidebells Penstemon pg. 199	*Penstemon segundiflorus*	4a–8b
Silvery Lupine pg. 201	*Lupinus argenteus*	3a–7b
Skyrocket Gilia pg. 203	*Ipomopsis aggregata*	2a–7b
Smooth Blue Aster pg. 205	*Symphyotrichum laeve*	4a–8b
Sticky Geranium pg. 207	*Geranium viscosissimum*	4a–9a
Streambank Wild Hollycock pg. 209	*Iliamana rivularis*	3a–8a
Sulphur Flower Buckwheat pg. 211	*Eriogonum umbellatum*	4a–8b
Three-nerved Goldenrod pg. 213	*Solidago velutina*	4a–7b
Tufted Evening Primrose pg. 215	*Oenothera cespitosa*	4a–10b
Western Red Columbine pg. 217	*Aquilegia formosa*	7a–10a
Western Sweetvetch pg. 219	*Hedysarum occidentale*	4a–8a
Western Wallflower pg. 221	*Erysimum capitatum*	4b–9b
Whipple's Penstemon pg. 223	*Penstemon whippleanus*	3a–7b
White Heath Aster pg. 225	*Symphyotrichum ericoides*	5a–10b
White Prairie-clover pg. 227	*Dalea candida*	3a–8b
Wild Bergamot pg. 229	*Monarda fistulosa*	3a–8b
Yellow Beeplant pg. 231	*Peritoma lutea*	5a–8b; grown as an annual in colder areas

ATTRACTS BUTTERFLIES	ATTRACTS BEES	ATTRACTS BIRDS	BLOOM PERIOD	DEER RESISTANT
nectar, host	yes	no	May–September	yes
nectar, host	yes	hummingbirds	May–July	yes
yes	yes	no	April–July	yes
yes	no	hummingbirds	May–September	yes
nectar, host	yes	no	August–October	yes
nectar, host	yes	seeds	May–August	yes
yes	yes	no	June–August	no
nectar, host	yes	seeds	April–September	yes
nectar, host	yes	no	July–October	yes
yes, especially sphinx moths	yes	no	April–September	yes
nectar, host	yes	hummingbirds	April–October	yes
yes	yes	seeds	June–August	yes
nectar, host	yes	seeds	March–September	yes
nectar, host	yes	hummingbirds	July–August	yes
nectar, host	yes	no	July–October	yes (mature)
nectar, host	yes	no	May–September	yes
yes, sphinx moths	yes	hummingbirds	June–August	yes
nectar, host	yes	seeds	May–August	yes

Rocky Mountain Plants at a Glance (continued)

COMMON NAME	SCIENTIFIC NAME	ROCKY MOUNTAIN HARDINESS ZONES
VINES & GROUNDCOVERS		
Bunchberry pg. 235	*Cornus canadensis*	4a–6a
Creeping Barberry pg. 237	*Berberis repens*	5b–7b
Kinnikinnick, Bearberry pg. 239	*Arctostaphylos uva-ursi*	2a–6b
Lanceleaf Stonecrop pg. 241	*Sedum lanceolatum*	4a–9b
Self-heal pg. 243	*Prunella vulgaris*	5a–9a
Silver Sage Wormwood pg. 245	*Artemisia ludoviciana*	4a–8b
Thicket Creeper pg. 247	*Parthenocissus vitacea*	4b–8b
Western Virgin's Bower pg. 249	*Clematis ligusticifolia*	5a–10b
GRASSES		
Alkali Sacaton pg. 253	*Sporobolus airoides*	4a–9b
Indian Ricegrass pg. 255	*Achnatherum hymenoides*	4a–7b
Purple Three-awn pg. 257	*Aristida purpurea*	6a–10b
Switchgrass pg. 259	*Panicum virgatum*	4a–9b

ATTRACTS BUTTERFLIES	ATTRACTS BEES	ATTRACTS BIRDS	BLOOM PERIOD	DEER RESISTANT
nectar, host	yes	fruit	May–July	yes
nectar, host (moths)	yes	no	April–June	yes
nectar, host	yes	fruit; hummingbirds	April–June; fruit: August–September	yes
nectar, host	shelter	no	May–September	yes
yes	yes	seeds	June–August	yes
host	no	no	July–October	yes
nectar, host	yes	fruit, shelter	June–August	yes
nectar, host	yes	shelter, nesting	July–September	yes
shelter, host	shelter	seeds	June–September	yes
host	shelter	seeds	July–September	no
host	shelter	no	April and October	yes
host	no	seeds	August	yes

Rocky Mountain Maple

Trees

Colorado Blue Spruce

Pinyon Pine

Quaking Aspen

Forests in the Rocky Mountains vary from foothill woodlands to mid-elevation montane forests to high-altitude subalpine forests. A large canopy tree requires 35 or more inches of annual precipitation. Many smaller trees favor riparian habitats with dependable water, while others thrive in the arid foothills. Many yards can easily duplicate these natural conditions with roof runoff or drip irrigation. Several small trees will provide food and shelter for birds and insect pollinators and host plants for butterflies and moths.

Gambel's Oak

Colorado Blue Spruce

Scientific Name *Picea pungens*

Family Pine (Pinaceae)

Plant Characteristics Evergreen pyramidal conifer reaching 10–40 feet tall in landscapes; leaves short, needlelike, blue-green; flowers wind-pollinated catkins; fruit slender cones. Deer, rabbit resistant.

USDA Hardiness Zones 2a–8a

Bloom Period Spring (April–May)

Growing Conditions Full sun to partial shade; rich, well-draining, regularly moist soil.

With its classic pyramidal shape and ornate blue-green foliage, Colorado blue spruce is one of the most beloved landscape trees of the Rocky Mountain region, and far beyond. More than 35 cultivars of varying size and colors ideal for specimen, screen, and windbreak plantings have been developed. But more than a landscape standout, it's an important all-around habitat tree. As a wind-pollinated conifer, it doesn't produce nectar to attract pollinators, but it is an important shelter tree. Most birds avoid perching in the open to evade predators, so they huddle in the shade and shelter of leafy shrubs and trees. A shelter tree near a bird feeder will significantly increase chickadee, goldfinch, kinglet, junco, and sparrow activity. Insects also seek shelter in trees. Caterpillars and pupating larva hide in the bark, leaves, and leaf litter, which supplies a major food source for birds, both while nesting and throughout the winter. Native to montane and subalpine forests, blue spruce typically needs extra water or the top 2 inches of soil will dry out.

Seed and shelter for birds, squirrels, and small mammals; larval host for up to 25 likely moth species fed upon by birds.

Gambel's Oak

Scientific Name *Quercus gambelii*

Family Beech (Fagaceae)

Plant Characteristics Deciduous, multi-trunked, thicket-forming shrub to small tree 12–25 feet tall; leaves deeply lobed, 2–7 inches long, turn red to yellow in fall; flowers wind-pollinated catkins 1½ inches long; acorns ¾ inch long. Foliage browsed by deer, rabbits.

USDA Hardiness Zones 4a–7b

Bloom Period Spring (March–April)

Growing Conditions Full sun; well-draining soil, drought tolerant once established.

Native to foothills into montane forests, this oak covers dry, fire-damaged slopes with dense thickets of head-high shrubby growth. With moderate water, like a garden setting, it develops into a handsome tree with a rounded crown. As a midsize specimen planting, Gambel's oak adds a dramatic accent to a front or backyard area. It provides summer shade and shelter for birds and butterflies, a crop of acorns for turkeys and other birds and many mammals, as well as caterpillars on the leaves and pupae in the furrowed bark that become bird food. Moth caterpillars on oaks are tremendously important as food for nestling songbirds. Prune young oaks to create a single trunk and rounded canopy, or let the root shoots spread into a bushy screen that presents a wall of brilliant fall colors. For a mixed woodland setting, pair with serviceberry, chokecherry, and snowberry.

Provides food, shelter, and nesting sites for birds; food for squirrels, chipmunks, and many small mammals; larval host for many moth species.

Pinyon Pine

Scientific Name *Pinus edulis*

Family Pine (Pinaceae)

Plant Characteristics Evergreen coniferous tree 20–40 feet tall with tapering-to-rounded crown; leaves short, needlelike, in bundles of 2; flowers wind-pollinated catkins; fruit a rounded cone with large, edible seeds. Deer, rabbit resistant.

USDA Hardiness Zones 5a–7b

Bloom Period Spring (April–May); cones take 2 years to mature

Growing Conditions Full sun to partial shade; coarse, well-draining soils.

Covering 4.8 million acres in Colorado alone, the pinyon-juniper woodlands are one of the keystone ecotypes of the West. The tree dominates the cool foothill transition zone between grasslands and montane forests. Though wind pollinated, pinyons perform a major ecological service in home habitat gardens. They supply shelter and nesting sites for birds and insects, and the large nuts feed birds, especially jays and ground-feeding species, and a myriad of small animals. In the spring, songbirds feed their nestlings caterpillars from the tree, and in the winter, chickadees and other bark-foraging birds feed on the pupae overwintering in the bark. Plant as a specimen tree for year-round foliage color and shade. It's smaller than many pines and develops into a picturesque tree suitable for side yards, back corners, and front yard plantings. Pinyons in nature commonly exceed 750 years in age.

Provides shelter and nesting sites for birds; seeds attract birds, squirrels, and small mammals; larval host for pine white butterfly (Neophasia menapia) and up to 14 moth species.

Ponderosa Pine

Scientific Name *Pinus ponderosa*

Family Pine (Pinaceae)

Plant Characteristics Evergreen coniferous tree, 60–100 feet tall in cultivation with a 20–30-foot spread, young trees have dark bark, older trees reddish-orange bark; needlelike leaves 5–10 inches long in bundles of 3; flowers catkins; cones oval, 4–6 inches long. Deer, rabbit resistant.

USDA Hardiness Zones 3a–7b

Bloom Period Spring (April)

Growing Conditions Full sun; light, moist, well-draining soils.

One of the tallest, most important trees of the Rockies, ponderosas grow into stately, large-scale specimens requiring ample room to develop their classic pyramidal crown and spreading limbs. As the tree develops, lower limbs can be removed to accent the classic orange bark and provide space for shade-tolerant understory wildflowers, grasses, and small shrubs. Fallen needles add a natural, slightly acidic mulch to the soil, ideal for many plants. The dense evergreen needles add a year-round foliage accent and provide critical shelter and nesting sites for birds, and the pine nuts provide food to birds and mammals. Many moths lay their eggs on the needles, and the larvae overwinter in the bark and ground litter around the trunk, providing a major food source for foraging birds.

Attracts numerous foliage and bark-foraging insectivorous and seed-eating birds; larval host for pine white butterfly (Neophasia menapia) and up to 14 moth species.

Quaking Aspen

Scientific Name *Populus tremuloides*

Family Willow (Salicaceae)

Plant Characteristics Deciduous tree with single or multiple, chalky-white trunks 20–50 feet tall and a narrow, rounded canopy; forms clonal colonies; leaves oval to triangular, 3 inches long, glossy green, turn red to gold in fall; flowers wind-pollinated catkins. Twigs, foliage, bark grazed by deer, rabbits.

USDA Hardiness Zones 1a–6b

Bloom Period Summer (June)

Growing Conditions Full sun; rich, moist, well-drained soils, needs extra water in hot exposures.

Aspens are considered the most widespread tree on the planet, but that's only one of their accomplishments. They spread by roots to form vast genetically identical colonies on mountainsides and meadows. The Pando aspen colony in Utah covers 100 acres with 40,000 trunks that weigh 13 million pounds and is estimated to be 15,000 years old, making it the biggest and oldest living organism in existence. Plant one in your habitat landscape and just think of the party conversation. More seriously, besides adding stunning year-round beauty to a landscape, aspens create shade and shelter for birds and insects and harbor dozens of species of butterfly and moth caterpillars. Plant several trees together to create your own colony. In the southern Rockies, aspens thrive above 7,000 feet with cool summers and deep, rich soil that receives a water surplus of at least 1 inch of runoff a year, so regular moisture is a must.

Food and shelter for birds; larval host for viceroy (Limenitis archippus) and western tiger swallowtail (Papilio rutulus) butterflies, as well as many moth species.

Rocky Mountain Maple

Scientific Name *Acer glabrum*

Family Horse-chestnut (Sapindaceae)

Plant Characteristics Deciduous, multi-stemmed, erect shrub 3–30 feet tall, occasionally single trunk; leaves large with 5–7 toothed lobes, turn brilliant reds, yellows in fall; flowers insignificant; seeds twin samaras with reddish wings. Deer, rabbit resistant.

USDA Hardiness Zones 4a–8b

Bloom Period Spring (April–May)

Growing Conditions Full sun to part shade; acidic, moist to dry, well-draining soils; summer irrigation at low elevations.

This dominant understory shrub performs best with cool summers, regularly moist soil, and full-to-moderate sun. It can be bushy or pruned into a large multi-stemmed shrub or medium-size tree with a single trunk. As a handsome addition to your habitat, it provides essential summer shade and shelter for birds, butterflies, and other insects, as well as nesting sites for songbirds. The reddish winged seeds add ornamental summer color and provide copious food for birds, squirrels, and other seed eaters. Then in the fall, the leaves turn brilliant hues of reds and yellows. Buy in containers and let them grow into your habitat space. Seeds require 6 months of cold treatment to germinate.

Attracts bees, the primary pollinators, and other small insects; larval host to western tiger swallowtail (Papilio rutulus), *mourning cloak* (Nymphalis antiopa).

Leadplant

Blue Elderberry

Shrubs

Shrubby Cinquefoil

Smooth Sumac

Common Snowberry

Chokecherry

Snakeweed, Broomweed

Woods' Rose

As one of the dominant plant types of most mountain ecosystems, shrubs should be a must for your pollinator garden. As woody perennials, they burst into bloom when the soil warms early in the spring. Shrubs provide early-season pollen and nectar for emerging insects, host plants for butterfly and moth larvae, and shelter and fruit for birds. As a bonus, many bloom off and on for three seasons, especially with periodic irrigation.

Gooseberry Currant

Rubber Rabbitbush

Alderleaf Mountain Mahogany

Scientific Name *Cercocarpus montanus*

Family Rose (Rosaceae)

Plant Characteristics Mostly deciduous shrub 3–12 feet tall with multiple erect, slender stems; leaves small, egg-shaped, veined; flowers tiny with a pink tube flared with yellowish lobes; fruit has a feathery, corkscrew-like tail. Not deer, rabbit resistant.

USDA Hardiness Zones 5a–9b

Bloom Period Spring (May–June)

Growing Conditions Full sun; coarse, dry, well-drained soils.

Caterpillars love to nibble the leaves of this native of shrublands, pinyon-juniper, and montane forests, leaving only slight damage and no problems. They add a living dimension to your habitat garden, especially the bizarre silk moth caterpillars. The adaptable alderleaf mountain mahogany develops a tall, slender vase-like shape suitable as a stand-alone profile accent, screen, background, or border. For xeriscaped natural areas, plant with antelope bitterbrush, rabbitbrush, snowberry, or fragrant sumac. The ornate feathery tails glow when backlit by the sun, then waft away in the breeze and corkscrew into the soil. The shrub is also called true and silverleaf mountain mahogany. Curl-leaf mountain mahogany (*C. ledifloius*) is also in the nursery trade.

Attracts butterflies, bees; larval host for mountain mahogany hairstreak (Satyrium tetra), Columbia silkmoth (Hyalophora columbia), and western sheepmoth (Hemileuca eglanterina).

Antelope Bitterbrush

Scientific Name *Purshia tridentata* var. *tridentata*

Family Rose (Rosaceae)

Plant Characteristics Upright to sprawling shrub, 3–6 feet tall and wide; small leaves persistent to winter deciduous with 3 teeth on tip; flowers white to creamy yellow, abundant along stems; fruit a 1-seeded capsule without a feathery tail. Foliage heavily browsed by deer, and young plants by rabbits, rodents.

USDA Hardiness Zones 5b–10a

Bloom Period Spring (March–June)

Growing Conditions Full sun, tolerates part shade; coarse, well-draining soils; heat and drought tolerant, water 1x/month in summer.

Native from Intermountain West sage scrublands to dry mountain slopes up to subalpine forests, this nitrogen-fixing shrub provides a robust addition to landscape habitats. In the early spring just as the leaves emerge, sweetly fragrant flowers blanket the branches and attract droves of insect pollinators. The intricate branching provides wildlife shelter, and birds feed on the seeds. The shrub often spreads wider than tall and may need pruning to keep a desired shape and size. Use in backgrounds, borders, or pruned in a hedge. It forms a colorful spring accent in naturalized areas or mixed plantings with rabbitbrush, sagebrush, and native ornamental grasses.

*Attracts many butterflies and bees and other pollinators; host plant for 10 confirmed and likely up to 22 butterfly and moth species, including the western sheepmoth (*Hemileuca eglanterina*); provides shelter and seeds for birds.*

Blue Elderberry

Scientific Name *Sambucus nigra* ssp. *cerulea*

Family Elderberry (Adoxaceae)

Plant Characteristics Deciduous shrub to small tree 6–12 feet tall with single or multiple ornate, branching trunks; small yellowish-white flowers in flat, 4–8-inch-wide clusters followed by blue-black drupes. Deer resistant.

USDA Hardiness Zones 6a–10b

Bloom Period Spring–summer (May–August); fruit: August–October

Growing Conditions Full sun to part shade and well-draining, moist soil.

Ideal for urban yards as accent or specimen plantings. Also called Mexican elderberry, this small-scale tree or dense shrub offers three-season benefits for pollinators and birds, plus long-lasting beauty for your yard. Large clusters of small, creamy flowers provide a rich source of nectar in the spring, and the blue-black berries feed birds in the fall. Additionally, the intricate branching and large compound leaves provide shade and perching and nesting shelter for birds. Native to drainages and stream sides, this moderately drought-tolerant plant needs additional water in hot, dry summers to keep its best appearance. Elderberries can flower the second year from seed and become shrub-sized in 3–4 years. They sucker from the base, so they may need regular pruning to shape and keep attractive. The berries, sweet when fully ripe, have many traditional food and medicinal uses, but red fruiting species are toxic.

Flowers attract hummingbirds, butterflies, bees, and other insect pollinators. Foliage provides shade, shelter, and nesting sites; seeds are an important late-summer food for birds.

Chokecherry

Scientific Name *Prunus virginiana*

Family Rose (Rosaceae)

Plant Characteristics Deciduous, thicket-forming, multi-branched shrub to small tree 3–20 feet tall and wide; leaves glossy green, oval, 1–4 inches long with finely-toothed edges, yellow to red in fall; small creamy flowers in elongated clusters 3–6 inches long; fruit a red-to-black drupe. Deer resistant.

USDA Hardiness Zones 5a–10b

Bloom Period Spring (May–June)

Growing Conditions Full sun, part shade; moist sandy, loam, clay, well-draining soil; summer water 2x/month.

Spreading by rhizomes, this native of chaparral and open woodlands welcomes wildlife with a feast of flowers, fruit, and foliage. Soon after spring leaves emerge, long tassels of pollen and nectar-rich flowers entice bees, the primary pollinators, and butterflies. Come summer, birds flock to devour the fleshy drupes, and the shiny green leaves host numerous butterfly and moth caterpillars. This garden-friendly pollinator keystone adds three-season beauty well into the fall when the leaves turn gold and red. Use as an accent shrub in a habitat island, understory fill-in, background screen, or hedge, or prune into a small tree for limited spaces. It partners well with snowberry, wild rose, red-osier dogwood, and currants. Cultivars with green leaves that age to purple and then turn red in autumn include 'Schubert' (a suckering tree) and 'Canada Red' (which doesn't sucker).

*Attracts bees, butterflies, and other pollinators; provides shelter and food for birds; larval host for western tiger swallowtail (*Papilio rutulus*), ceanothus silkmoth (*Hyalophora euryalus*), and up to 122 butterfly and moth species.*

Cliffbush

Scientific Name *Jamesia americana*

Family Hydrangea (Hydrangeaceae)

Plant Characteristics Deciduous, upright-to-rounded shrub 4–6 feet tall and wide with brown, shredding bark, short branches; small, oval-toothed leaves; and dense, rounded clusters of showy white flowers. Deer resistant.

USDA Hardiness Zones 3a–8b

Bloom Period Spring (May–June)

Growing Conditions Performs best in part shade, tolerates full sun; coarse, well-draining soils; heat and drought tolerant, summer water 2x/month will enhance growth, flowering.

Native to shaded canyons and slopes, this midsize shrub bursts into bloom in the spring with rounded clusters of fragrant, white flowers; provides a summer green accent with ornate, toothed leaves; and then turns brilliant shades of red and orange in the fall. It's a three-season showoff, perfect as an understory shrub in dappled sunlight or as a small-space accent. It pairs well with mountainspray, snowberry, and mock orange. Smaller shrubs like Woods' rose, currants, and thimbleberry add a basal layer of color interest. Though it survives drought conditions, it thrives with regular irrigation, especially in sunny locations, and grows and flowers vigorously.

Attracts butterflies, bees, bumblebees, and other insect pollinators; larval host for white-lined sphinx moth (Hyles lineata); shelter for birds.

Cliff Fendlerbush

Scientific Name *Fendlera rupicola*

Family Hydrangea (Hydrangeaceae)

Plant Characteristics Deciduous, 3–6 feet tall to 4 feet wide, rounded to vase-shaped with multiple branches and reddish-tan bark; small, narrow leaves, white flowers blanket branch tips. Browsed by deer.

USDA Hardiness Zones 4a–7b

Bloom Period Spring (April–June)

Growing Conditions Full sun; coarse, well-draining soils; no supplemental water once established.

Favoring dry, rocky pinyon-juniper foothills and mountain shrub habitats, this heat and drought tolerant, midsize shrub is custom made for xeriscape palettes. In the spring, it accents xeric gardens with a profusion of snow-white to pink-tinted, 1–2-inch-wide flowers. It's ideal as a specimen or background plant, or use it as a color accent in a naturalized area. Companions for mixed wildscape plantings include serviceberry, fragrant sumac, snakeweed, and antelope bitterbrush. To maintain size and branch density, prune after flowering because it blooms on the previous year's growth.

Attracts numerous bees, butterflies, moths, and native flies; shelter for birds.

Common Snowberry

Scientific Name *Symphoricarpos albus* var. *laevigatus*

Family Honeysuckle (Caprifoliaceae)

Plant Characteristics Rounded, branching, deciduous shrub 3–6 feet tall and wide, thicket forming; leaves blue-green, oval 1–2 inches long; flowers small, pinkish-white, bell-shaped, in short, tight clusters; fruit a pearl-sized, white drupe. Deer resistant.

USDA Hardiness Zones 5a–9b

Bloom Period Spring, Summer (May–July); fruit: Fall, Winter

Growing Conditions Full sun, part shade; coarse, loamy, or clay, well-drained soil; water 1–3x/month once established.

Native to mountains and foothill woodlands, this spreading, thicket-forming shrub develops dense branches with arching stems in full sun, but easily nestles beneath trees. Hummingbirds and bees love the pink flowers, but the real garden highlight comes in the winter when dense clusters of marble-sized, snow-white drupes dangle on the limbs. Plant snowberry as a hedge, background, mixed border, or understory accent. Partner with thimbleberry, currants, gooseberries, and Woods' rose. Spreads by rhizomes; sheer to size in winter or severely prune to rejuvenate. Common snowberry shares its southern range with roundleaf snowberry (*S. rotundifolius*) with trumpet-shaped flowers and the same habitat gardening applications.

*Attracts butterflies, bees, hummingbirds, and other pollinators; provides bird shelter; larval host for checkerspot butterflies (*Euphydryas *species), western sheepmoth (*Hemileuca eglanterina*), and up to 28 other moth species.*

Fragrant Sumac

Scientific Name *Rhus aromatica (tribolata)*
Family Sumac (Anacardaceae)
Plant Characteristics Deciduous, spreading, multi-branched, thicket-forming shrub 3–6 feet tall and wide; leaves compound with 3 leaflets, pungent, orange in fall; tiny flowers before leaves emerge; fruit clusters of sticky red drupes. Deer resistant.
USDA Hardiness Zones 5a–10b
Bloom Period Spring (March–May); fruit: July–October
Growing Conditions Best in full sun, tolerates part shade; coarse, well-draining soil; water 1x/month once established.

Native from dry rocky slopes and moist canyons to mixed conifer montane forests, this widespread shrub provides three seasons of premier pollinator benefits and garden colorscaping. The tiny yellow flowers on bare stems are inconspicuous, except to the bees who dive in for an all-important early-spring source of nectar. Clusters of ornamental red fruit decorate the compact shrub in the summer and feed the birds. Come autumn, the leaves turn hues of orange and red for a burst of brilliant garden color. Partner it with flowering evergreens as a foliage accent for borders, background hedges, or slope plantings. The 2–3-foot-high 'Gro–Low' cultivars are suitable for walkways, medians, and groundcovers. Male and female sumac plants are separate, so you'll need both to get fruit. Prune to size in the winter to keep it compact and dense.

Flowers attract bees, native flies; larval host for up to 20 butterfly and moth species; provides seeds and shelter for birds.

Golden Currant

Scientific Name *Ribes aureum*

Family Gooseberry (Grossulariaceae)

Plant Characteristics Winter deciduous shrub 3–6 feet tall and wide with multiple, thornless stems from base; leaves pale-green, rounded with 3 lobes; flowers yellow, tubular, clustered in leaf axils along branches; berries red, orange, or black. Deer resistant.

USDA Hardiness Zones 5a–10b; cold hardy to -38° F.

Bloom Period April–June

Growing Conditions Full sun to part shade; fine-to-coarse, loamy, well-draining soil; water 1–2x/month in summer.

With fragrant, golden-yellow, early spring flowers and abundant summer berries, this plant has exceptionally high wildlife value, especially for hummingbirds, songbirds, and monarch butterflies. Add its ornate, lobed leaves that turn hues of burgundy in the fall and you have a premier plant for your pollinator garden. Currants spread by rhizomes and can form a thick background against a wall, along a border, or as an understory fill-in or groundcover. They accent an oval garden or courtyard, or they can be trimmed into a well-foliated container plant. They naturally occur along streams from plains to mid-elevation woodlands, so summer water keeps them robust, and fall pruning maintains the desired size and dense branching. Nurseries carry several varieties and cultivars.

Attracts hummingbirds, butterflies, bumblebees, long-tongued bees; birds eat the berries; larval host for up to 80 butterflies and moth species.

Gooseberry Currant

Scientific Name *Ribes montigenum*

Family Gooseberry (Grossulariaceae)

Plant Characteristics Deciduous, spreading stems 1–4 feet tall have spines and prickles; leaves small, irregularly 5-lobed; flower clusters pendent with 3–8 bell-shaped, red-to-pink flowers; berries bright red with few dark hairs. Deer and rabbit resistant.

USDA Hardiness Zones 4a–7a

Bloom Period Summer (June–August)

Growing Conditions Partial shade at mid elevations; coarse, well-draining soils; water 1–2x/month once established.

With showy clusters of tubular red flowers and bright-red berries, this currant is native to mid- to high-elevation forests and alpine slopes. In a mid-elevation garden setting, it creates an eye-catching spring and summer accent. It's well armed with spines, so use in spots with little human contact, such as naturalized areas, backgrounds, or back borders. With showy spring flowers and delicious summer fruit, gooseberry currant is a sure crowd-pleaser in a wildlife pollinator garden.

Flowers attract butterflies, bees, bumblebees, hummingbirds; larval host for up to 79 butterfly and moth species; birds feed on berries.

Leadplant

Scientific Name *Amorpha canescens*

Family Legume (Fabaceae)

Plant Characteristics Upright deciduous shrub 1–3 feet tall and wide, with open branching; compound leaves have 13–20 narrow, gray-green, white-hairy leaflets; vertical spikes packed with small purple flowers. Deer and rabbit resistant.

USDA Hardiness Zones 4a–7b

Bloom Period Spring–summer (May–July)

Growing Conditions Full sun, tolerates part shade; needs well-draining soil.

Butterflies and bees love the vibrant masses of 3–8-inch-long spikes of purple flowers highlighted with a cover of contrasting yellow stamens. Fast growing, this upright, open-branching shrub will fill an empty space in a corner or along a wall, add a vertical element to a background planting, or bring fine-textured foliage and color to mixed border plantings. The airy gray-green foliage and spikes of purple flowers complement mixed border and background plantings and naturalized areas. Birds use the leafy branches for cover. Native to foothills and the High Plains, it does well in Front Range gardens, requiring minimal supplemental landscape water. You can size it for small gardens or shape as a medium-size shrub for a hedge or specimen planting; prune severely if it gets leggy.

Attracts butterflies, bees, and other insect pollinators; larval host plant for silver spotted skipper (Epargyreus clarus), *gray hairstreak* (Strymon melinus), *northern cloudywing* (Thorybes pylades), *and southern dogface* (Zerene cesonia) *butterflies, and several moth species.*

Lewis Mock Orange

Scientific Name *Philadelphus lewisii*

Family Hydrangea (Hydrageaceae)

Plant Characteristics Deciduous, erect-to-rounded shrub 4–9 feet tall with multiple, branching stems; leaves opposite, lance-shaped to elliptic, 1–2 inches long, soft yellow in fall; dense clusters on branch tips, flowers 1–1½ inches wide with 4 snow-white, oblong petals. Deer, rabbit resistant.

USDA Hardiness Zones 4a–9b

Bloom Period Summer (May–July)

Growing Conditions Full sun to partial shade; dry to moist, well-draining soils.

In spring, these bushy shrubs with long, arching branches look like a late-season snowstorm. Clusters of fragrant white flowers nearly obscure the soft green leaves, attracting butterflies, bumblebees, and bees. Use as an accent specimen, border, foundation hedge, or to enliven a naturalized woodland area. Native to moist slopes, valleys, and woodlands from shrub- and grasslands to montane forests in the northern Rockies, it makes an eye-catching addition to a pollinator habitat. Light pruning will keep it dense and full. It's the state flower of Idaho. Various species, cultivars, and hybrids are in the trade, so be sure to get a plant adapted to your region. In Utah, Colorado, and New Mexico, little-leaf mock orange (*P. microphyllus*) replaces Lewis.

Attracts butterflies, bees, bumblebees; larval host for 3 moth species.

Mountain Ninebark

Scientific Name *Physocarpus monogynus*

Family Rose (Rosaceae)

Plant Characteristics Deciduous, compact shrub 2–4 feet tall and wide with bark peeling in strips; small, lobed, toothed leaves; showy, rounded clusters of ½-inch-wide white flowers. Deer resistant.

USDA Hardiness Zones 4a–8b

Bloom Period Summer (May–July)

Growing Conditions Full sun to part shade; coarse, well-draining soils; occasional to moderate water.

This small-scale shrub is native to canyons and slopes from the foothills to mixed conifer forests. In a garden, it adapts to sun or part shade and moderately dry conditions. When covered with flower clusters, ninebark creates an eye-catching focal point, and then a dense, green foliage accent through the summer. For a mixed border or low hedge, team with cliffbush, Woods' rose, or shrubby cinquefoil. To promote dense branching, prune divergent branches after flowering because it blooms on new growth. To rejuvenate, cut back old stems severely. In the summer, the inflated, reddish-brown capsules split to provide seeds for birds.

Attracts butterflies, bees, and other insect pollinators; provides shelter and food for birds.

Mountainspray

Scientific Name *Holodiscus discolor (dumosus)*

Family Rose (Rosaceae)

Plant Characteristics Deciduous, multi-stemmed shrub to small tree 5–18 feet tall and wide with slender arching branches; leaves gray-green, oval, 1–3 inches long with toothed margins; small creamy flowers in dense pyramidal sprays 4–10 inches long and wide on branch tips; seeds tiny, wind dispersed. Deer resistant.

USDA Hardiness Zones 5b–7b

Bloom Period Summer (May–August)

Growing Conditions Part shade, tolerates shade; coarse, gravelly, loamy, well-draining soils; water 2x/month once established, needs summer water.

Mountainspray is common to forest openings and understories, this fast-growing shrub thrives in part shade. In the spring, spectacular clusters of creamy flowers are butterfly-and-bee magnets and eye-catching garden accents. Heavy with frothy flowers, the branches usually droop, giving the plant its common name. It adds fall color with yellow-to-red leaves. Use in backgrounds, as an understory accent, along walls, or in mixed plantings. It's a good companion for red-osier dogwood, red elderberry, chokecherry, and mock orange, or use it as a color accent underplanted beneath Woods' rose, shrubby cinquefoil, or currants. Prune occasionally after flowering to maintain a loose, graceful shrub, and trim off the spent brown flower clusters for a manicured look.

Attracts butterflies, bees, and other insect pollinators; provides shelter for birds; larval host for up to 37 butterfly and moth species.

Red Elderberry

Scientific Name *Sambucus racemosa*

Family Elderberry (Adoxaceae)

Plant Characteristics Deciduous bushy shrub or small tree, multi-branched from base, 3–12 feet tall and wide; leaves compound with toothed leaflets; showy rounded clusters of small, white flowers are followed by bright-red, bitter drupes (or black in var. *melanocarpa*). Moderately resistant to deer, rabbits.

USDA Hardiness Zones 3a–7b

Bloom Period Spring–summer (March–July)

Growing Conditions Full sun to part shade; rich, well-drained soils, regularly moist.

Native to stream sides and wet meadows in coniferous forests, red elderberry creates a striking ornamental addition to a habitat garden. Large clusters of creamy flowers attract pollinators; brilliant red fruit decorates the plant through the summer, until birds, deer, and small animals devour it; and the large leaves provide a dense green foliage accent and wildlife shelter. The rounded-to-sprawling shape is suitable for a background or wall accent, a hedge, and in naturalized areas. It's adaptable but thrives best in rich soil with regular moisture. Prune in winter to maintain dense foliage and desired shape, and rejuvenate with a hard pruning.

Attracts butterflies, bees, native flies; host for up to 23 butterfly and moth species; provides food, shelter for songbirds and game birds.

Red-osier Dogwood

Scientific Name *Cornus sericea*

Family Dogwood (Cornaceae)

Plant Characteristics Deciduous shrub with multiple wand-like stems 3–10 feet tall, leafless stems turn red in winter; bright-green leaves 2–4 inches long, oval, pointed, prominent veins; small white flowers form showy clusters; fruit small white drupes in showy clusters. Deer palatable.

USDA Hardiness Zones 5a–10b

Bloom Period Spring–summer (April–June)

Growing Conditions Part shade to full shade; moist, loamy medium- to slow-draining soils; water 1x/week once established.

This open-branching shrub naturally grows as an understory shrub along streams, so in a habitat garden it thrives in dappled shade and regular irrigation. Make it happy and it will provide year-round color and three seasons of forage and cover for wildlife. In the spring, bees, butterflies, and moths feast on the showy clusters of creamy flowers, then come summer, birds devour the fleshy, white drupes. The dense foliage provides nesting and shelter for birds. The ornate leaves turn hues of yellow and orange in the fall, then drop to reveal a multi-stemmed matrix of red branches and twigs that provides a vivid color accent all winter. Use as a background plant, a wall accent, landscape island anchor, or as a year-round color accent for patios, courtyards, and walls. This dogwood spreads by rhizomes and can form colonies in loose, garden soils. Also called creek and American dogwood.

Attracts butterflies, bees, moths, and other insects; larval host for up to 42 moth species; fruit relished by birds.

Rubber Rabbitbrush

Scientific Name *Ericameria nauseosa*

Family Aster (Asteraceae)

Plant Characteristics Evergreen, rounded shrub 3–6 feet tall and wide; leaves gray-green, woolly-hairy, thread-like; flat-topped flower clusters to 4 inches wide have small yellow flower heads with disk florets only; fall blooming. Deer, rabbit resistant.

USDA Hardiness Zones 4a–9b

Bloom Period Summer–fall (July–October)

Growing Conditions Performs best in full sun; needs sandy, gravelly, well-draining soil.

From late summer through fall, dense arrays of small yellow flowers transform this rounded shrub into a mound of gold. As a semi-evergreen (ever-gray) specimen plant with soft-textured, silvery-ashen foliage and brilliant fall color, rabbitbrush provides an attractive year-round accent. Its dominant, spreading size especially adapts it for backgrounds, unsheared hedges along fences and walls, and as a wildlife cover for naturalized areas. It pairs well with ornate grasses and smaller bushy shrubs like snakeweed. Winter pruning keeps this fast-growing shrub properly sized and densely foliated. Or you can prune the lower stems to create a shrub with gnarled trunks. It spreads, especially in disturbed soils, by self-seeding. Rabbitbrush naturally grows from mid-elevation, semi-desert grasslands and sagebrush with medium moisture into high mountains. Over 20 varieties have been described throughout the West, some with green, not gray, foliage. Also commonly called chamisa.

Highly attractive to butterflies, bees, and many other insect pollinators; larval host to sagebrush checkerspot (Chlosyne acastus).

Shrubby Cinquefoil

Scientific Name *Dasiphora fruticosa*

Family Rose (Rosaceae)

Plant Characteristics Deciduous shrub, densely branching, low-mounding 1–3 feet tall and wide; small, compound, silky-hairy leaves; showy, bright-yellow flowers 1 inch wide. Deer, rabbit resistant.

USDA Hardiness Zones 3b–7b

Bloom Period Summer–fall (June–September)

Growing Conditions Full sun, tolerates part shade; well-draining, regularly irrigated soil.

Native from the foothills to alpine meadows, this adaptable, small-scale shrub is right at home in garden settings. The small size suits foreground plantings, walkways and patio accents, and even mass plantings as a border hedge or ground cover. The abundant, long-blooming flowers create an eye-catching splash of color all summer. The saucer-shaped flowers are a nectar bonanza for butterflies and bees throughout the summer. Water regularly and protect from blazing sun at lower elevations. Trim in winter to maintain size and density and to promote vigorous blooming on new growth. Cultivars have flowers with shades of yellow to white.

Attracts large numbers of butterflies and bees; recorded host for at least 9 butterfly and moth species.

Smooth Sumac

Scientific Name *Rhus glabra*

Family Sumac (Anacardiaceae)

Plant Characteristics Deciduous shrub or small tree 4–12 feet tall, thicket forming; compound leaves have a reddish midrib with 13–31 lance-shaped leaflets, scarlet in the fall; large, dense, pyramidal clusters of small, creamy flowers on branch tips produce clusters of red drupes; male and female plants separate.

USDA Hardiness Zones 3a–9b

Bloom Period Summer (June–August); ornate fruits may overwinter

Growing Conditions Performs best in full sun, tolerates light shade; needs average-to-rich, well-draining soil.

If you have enough space, the fast-growing, multi-stemmed sumac adds three-season color while fulfilling multiple wildlife needs. In the spring, showy clusters of creamy-white flowers attract numerous species of native bees and butterflies. During the hot summer, the leafy branches provide light shade and shelter for birds. Then after a vivid display of scarlet fall-leaf color, showy clusters of red drupes feed birds through the winter. Smooth sumacs spread by rhizomes and form crowded shrubby- to tree-sized colonies, which can make an attractive addition or become a nuisance. Male plants produce both nectar and pollen and attract the most bees; females offer only nectar but also provide seeds for birds. Several trees of each sex are required to ensure the females get seeds. Smooth sumacs are well suited for poor soils, naturalized areas where they can spread, corner or back-lot fills, or accents against border walls.

Attracts bees, butterflies, moths, and other insect pollinators; larval host plant for many butterfly and moth species; winter food for birds.

Snakeweed, Broomweed

Scientific Name *Gutierrezia sarothrae*

Family Aster (Asteraceae)

Plant Characteristics Rounded, spreading evergreen subshrub 1–3 feet tall and wide with thin, densely-branched stems; bright-green leaves are short, narrow, and crowded on stems; dense clusters of flower heads on stem tips have 3–8 small yellow rays and a yellow disk; in bloom, they blanket the plant and obscure the leaves.

USDA Hardiness Zones 3a–10b

Bloom Period Summer–fall (July–November)

Growing Conditions Performs best in full sun and sandy, gravelly, well-draining soils.

Equally at home in desert scrublands and high mountain slopes from Mexico to Canada, this well-mannered basketball-size shrublet will win your respect, and heart, when it bursts into flamboyant bloom. Besides delighting all manner of pollinators, its dense cover of golden flowers adds late-season color to garden foregrounds, borders, and naturalized areas. For a long-blooming groundcover or a fill-in, team snakeweed with purple prairie-clover, purple aster, or gayfeather. Too much shade and it becomes weak and lanky, too much water and it dies, so withhold the TLC and watch it thrive. In coarse, low-organic soils, snakeweed readily self-seeds and blooms the first year. You can trim the brown winter seed heads for a tidy look, or wait and see how the fresh spring growth quickly covers the spent heads.

Highly attractive to butterflies, bees, and many other insect pollinators; larval host for many butterfly and moth species.

Thimbleberry

Scientific Name *Rubus parviflorus*

Family Rose (Rosaceae)

Plant Characteristics Deciduous, spreading, leafy shrub 3–6 feet tall, thornless; large, lobed, maple-like leaves, orange fall color; clusters of white, 2-inch-wide flowers; raspberry-like red fruit; colony forming. Deer, rabbit resistant.

USDA Hardiness Zones 4a–6b

Bloom Period Summer (May–August)

Growing Conditions Partial shade, shade; rich, well-draining soils; water 1x/month once established.

Native to conifer forest openings and edges, this colony-forming shrub lends a dense, bushy three-season accent to a wildscape or naturalized area, border or background planting, or even a container focal point. Spring flowers attract bees and butterflies, summer fruit feeds birds, and the fall leaves turn rich shades of reds and yellows. It spreads by roots, so it's popular for slope erosion control or a forest-setting groundcover. Prune in winter to maintain size and shape.

Flowers attract butterflies and bees, fruit supplies food for songbirds and game birds; host plant for up to 70 butterfly and moth species.

Twinberry Honeysuckle

Scientific Name *Lonicera involucrata*

Family Honeysuckle (Caprifoliaceae)

Plant Characteristics Deciduous bushy shrub 3–9 feet tall, 4–5 feet wide; bright-green leaves elliptic, 2–5 inches long; flowers paired, tubular, yellow, ¾ inch long; fruit ½ inch diameter, black berry. Deer resistant.

USDA Hardiness Zones 5a–10b

Bloom Period Summer (June–July)

Growing Conditions Full sun, part shade; moist, sandy, loamy, well-draining soil; summer water 1x/week once established.

Occurring in open-edge habitats in periodically damp soils, this densely foliated shrub will be happy in a similar garden habitat, and so will the birds and insect pollinators. In the spring, the paired tubular flowers attract hummingbirds, butterflies, bees; then in the summer, birds devour the juicy fruit. This underrated ornamental adds bright-green foliage color and cover for birds, then by late summer, the leaf-like bracts around the blue-black berries turn a dark red for a striking green-red-black color contrast. Use as a garden background, wall border, summer screen, slope planting, or ornamental specimen. It pairs well with ninebark, mountainspray, currants, and red-osier dogwood.

Attracts hummingbirds, butterflies, bees, many other insects; provides food and cover for birds; larval host for variable checkerspot (Euphydryas chalcedona) and up to 25 other butterfly and moth species.

Western Mountain Ash

Scientific Name *Sorbus sitchensis*

Family Rose (Rosaceae)

Plant Characteristics Deciduous, spreading shrub 3–15 feet tall with multiple stems; leaves large, compound, shiny green, red in fall; small white flowers form large, flat-topped clusters; fruit a small fleshy, red-to-orange, bitter drupe. Foliage browsed by deer.

USDA Hardiness Zones 2a–7b

Bloom Period Spring (March–June)

Growing Conditions Sun to part shade; rich, well-draining soils; regular moisture.

Native to open forests, rocky hillsides, and riparian areas at mid-to-high elevations, mountain ash adds a distinct forest flavor to a habitat garden. The densely mounding plant is suitable as a background cover, border hedge, in naturalized areas, or a stand-alone yard specimen. It provides three-season appeal: flowers blanket the shrub in the spring, ornate red berries highlight the dense green foliage through the summer, and the leaves turn fiery reds and oranges in the fall. The bright fruit remains on the plant into the winter, or until songbirds, game birds, and mammals devour them. Prune in winter to maintain desired size and shape.

Attracts butterflies, bees, and other insect pollinators; larval host for up to 23 butterfly and moth species; important food source for birds and mammals.

Western Serviceberry

Scientific Name *Amelanchier alnifolia*

Family Rose (Rosaceae)

Plant Characteristics Deciduous upright shrub to small tree 3–16 feet tall with intricate branching, small oval leaves, clusters of showy white flowers 1 inch wide that emerge before or with leaves, and fleshy berry-like, purple fruit; colony forming. Browsed by deer.

USDA Hardiness Zones 4a–7b

Bloom Period Summer (May–July)

Growing Conditions Well-draining, coarse, occasionally moist soils; full sun to part shade. Water 1–2x/month once established.

Wide ranging from sagebrush plains to aspen and spruce-fir forests, this adaptable shrub attracts pollinators with dense arrays of brilliant white flowers, and it welcomes birds with abundant summer fruit. Intricate branching and dense foliage also provide cover and nesting for birds. With orange-to-red fall colors, serviceberry adds a three-season accent to corner, border, or mixed groupings. Dense branching adapts it to mixed hedges, screens, or specimen plantings. Small- to medium-size cultivars have been developed with compact branching. Prune during winter dormancy to maintain a compact shape and to promote flowering on new growth. Utah serviceberry (*A. utahensis*) has similar landscaping applications.

Flowers attract butterflies, bees, and other pollinators; larval host for likely up to 54 other butterflies and moths, including hairstreaks, admirals, and swallowtails; provides bird food and shelter.

White Spirea

Scientific Name *Spiraea betulifolia*

Family Rose, Rosaceae

Plant Characteristics Deciduous dwarf shrub with single or multiple stems 1–3 feet tall and wide, may freeze to ground in winter; leaves egg-shaped, toothed, 2 inches long and turn quality orange, red, magenta in fall; dense, flat-topped clusters are packed with tiny white flowers. Deer, rabbit resistant.

USDA Hardiness Zones 5a–8b

Bloom Period Summer (May–July)

Growing Conditions Full sun to part shade; regularly moist, well-draining soils.

Native to moist montane woodlands and meadows from Wyoming to Canada, this low-growing shrub is great for walkway borders, foundation hedges, backgrounds, or specimen plantings. It spreads by rhizomes and can colonize open areas. Butterflies, bees, and beetles particularly love the long-lasting, nectar-pollen-rich flowers. After a summer of blooming, the leaves add stunning color to your landscape. Like all rose family species, it blooms on new growth, so prune in winter or after spring blooming. Stems may die to the ground in winter. Numerous selections, hybrids, and introduced species exist with blue-green and yellowish-green leaves (and pink flowers), so be sure to get one adapted to your area. Also called white meadowsweet and birchleaf spirea.

Highly attractive to butterflies, bees; larval host for up to 35 butterfly and moth species.

Woods' Rose

Scientific Name *Rosa woodsii*

Family Rose (Rosaceae)

Plant Characteristics Deciduous, densely branching, thicket-forming shrub with thorny stems 3–6 feet tall and wide, depending on variety; compound leaves have 5–9 oval, toothed leaflets; clusters of showy 2-inch-wide, fragrant flowers have 5 pink-to-red petals and many showy yellow stamens; fruit is an orange-red hip filled with seeds.

USDA Hardiness Zones 4a–8a

Bloom Period Spring–summer (April–August)

Growing Conditions Performs best in full sun, tolerates part shade; needs moderately fertile, loamy, well-draining, moist to semidry soil.

Plant this fast-growing native rose for its gorgeous displays of light-pink-to-deep-red flowers, followed by bright, orange-red hips. But keep your shears handy to control the size and shape. In riparian areas in nature, it can form 6-foot-tall thickets with thorny stems. In high-altitude forests, it remains an open-branching understory subshrub. In lush garden settings, it will strive to reach its full potential, so resist too much TLC. Prune in the winter, then enjoy the spring parade of bees and other insects. It accents patio and window-view gardens, foundation plantings, and landscape islands. It adds a color focal point to mixed hedges and border plantings when paired with tarbush, rabbitbrush, or chokecherry. It naturally occurs in periodically moist soils at mid-elevations and higher, so it needs little supplemental irrigation.

*Highly attractive to bees, butterflies, and many other insect pollinators; larval host for Columbia silkmoth (*Hyalophora columbia*) and up to 54 butterfly and moth species.*

Pearly Everlasting

Scarlet Globemallow

Whipple's Penstemon

Wildflowers

Dwarf Larkspur

Showy Fleabane

Black-eyed Susan

Cutleaf Anemone

Choosing wildflowers for your pollinator garden is where you can let your imagination and creativity run wild. Their beauty and diversity can bring joy with every new bud that pops open and every butterfly and bee that stops by for a sip of nectar. Select perennials for dependable year-after-year blooms, but don't neglect of annuals. In a rush to bloom and set seed with the spring rains, they can blanket your garden with a riot of color. Consider color and size combinations, coordinated bloom times, and mass or fill-in plantings.

Narrow Bluebells

Showy Milkweed

Butterfly Milkweed

Black-eyed Susan

Scientific Name *Rudbeckia hirta*

Family Aster (Asteraceae)

Plant Characteristics Upright herbaceous annual, biennial, or short-lived perennial 1–3 feet tall; grayish-green leaves are lance-shaped and covered with short, rough hairs; 2–3-inch-wide flower heads have showy yellow rays around a domed brown center. Deer, rabbit resistant.

USDA Hardiness Zones 3a–7b

Bloom Period Summer (June–September)

Growing Conditions Performs best in full sun, tolerates light shade; needs moist-to-dry, well-drained garden soil.

Native and naturalized in open, mid-elevation habitats throughout much of the Rockies, black-eyed Susan makes a bold color statement when mass planted as a garden background or wall border, in landscape islands, or in open wildscape areas. The long-lasting, nectar- and pollen-rich flowers attract pollinators throughout the hot summer months. It pairs well with the similar-sized butterfly milkweed, prairie-clovers, and coneflower. It will need a weekly deep watering in dry summer periods to maintain blooming and prime condition. Plant seedlings and sow seeds in the spring after the last frost for summer blooms. It readily self-seeds, so resist deadheading all the mature flowers and you'll have a flamboyant colony year after year. Cultivars with reddish centers are available.

Highly attractive to butterflies, bees, and many other short- and long-tongued insect pollinators; larval host for the silver checkerspot butterfly (Chlosyne nycteis).

Blanket Flower

Scientific Name *Gaillardia aristata*

Family Aster (Asteraceae)

Plant Characteristics Upright herbaceous annual 1–2 feet tall; leafy rosettes and scattered stem leaves are lance-shaped with edges smooth to lobed or toothed; flower heads 2 inches wide, rays vary from solid yellow, yellow with a red base, to bright red with yellow tips; disk maroon to brown. Deer, rabbit resistant.

USDA Hardiness Zones 4a–7b

Bloom Period Spring–fall (April–October–frost)

Growing Conditions Performs best in full sun, tolerates part shade; needs coarse, well-draining soil.

Native from plains to montane forest, this is the flower that keeps on giving. Flush with multicolored red-and-yellow flowers from spring until first frost, it supplies flamboyant color to your garden and your dining-table bouquets, nectar and pollen for pollinators, and seeds for birds. Mass plant it for a naturalized wave of color, in tidy groups for spot color, along borders and medians, as fill-in plants for patio gardens and containers, and accents in oval gardens. In other words, you can't go wrong with this drought-tolerant favorite. This short-lived perennial readily self-seeds. Sow seeds directly in the ground after the last frost or several weeks earlier in starter pots. Deadhead during the spring and summer to prolong blooming, then let them go to seed in the fall for next year's crop. Sow seeds anytime.

Highly attractive to butterflies, bees, and many other insect pollinators; birds feed on the seeds.

Blue Flax

Scientific Name *Linum lewisii*

Family Flax (Linaceae)

Plant Characteristics Upright herbaceous perennial with open branching and slender stems 1–3 feet tall; small leaves are linear to lance-shaped; light- to dark-blue flowers; 1 inch wide, bloom in the morning and fade by afternoon, new buds open every day.

USDA Hardiness Zones 4b–9b

Bloom Period Spring–summer (March–July)

Growing Conditions Performs best in full sun, tolerates dappled shade; needs dry sandy, loamy, well-draining soil.

Tall, slender stems have wand-like branches covered with scores of delicate blue flowers that add a colorful, airy texture in a mixed planting. Use it to brighten up sunny borders and patio gardens. For a dramatic, three-season colorscape, mix the sky-blue flowers with a palette of blanket flower, western wallflower, and Rocky Mountain penstemon. Sow seeds for a mass-planted window garden and enjoy the bee and butterfly activity all morning. The flowers fade by afternoon, but the nodding buds beneath the flowers are ready to pop the next morning. Flowers vary in intensity of blue and have dark guidelines to lead bees to the yellow throat. Blue flax naturally grows from grasslands to conifer forests, so a few monthly deep drinks will help maintain profuse blooming. It is a short-lived perennial that readily reseeds on open ground, so you should be able to enjoy the dainty flowers for springs to come. Cultivars of blue flax are included in many seed mixes, often the 'Appar' variety that is deep blue and blooms for six weeks. Also known as prairie flax.

*Attracts butterflies, bees, and many other insect pollinators; larval host for variegated fritillary butterfly (*Euptoieta claudia*).*

Butterfly Milkweed

Scientific Name *Asclepias tuberosa*

Family Dogbane (Apocynaceae)

Plant Characteristics Upright taprooted, hairy, herbaceous perennial 1½–3 feet tall; leaves narrow and hairy; small flowers yellow to orange, in dense, flat clusters 2–5 inches wide; fruit a narrow, erect pod; sap is clear and watery. Deer and rabbit resistant.

USDA Hardiness Zones 3a–9b

Bloom Period Spring–summer (May–September)

Growing Conditions Performs best in full sun, tolerates part shade; needs natural, coarse, well-draining soil.

Butterflies and hummingbirds, as well as bees and all sorts of nectar-loving insects, flock to this flamboyant accent in a pollinator garden. Butterfly milkweed often grows along drainages in mid-elevation woodlands, so in hot, arid locales it benefits from weekly water and relief from the blazing afternoon sun. Most literature says you must wait 2–3 years from seed to bloom, but I've had it flower the first year. It mixes well with other milkweeds and complements yellow and red flowering plants. This long bloomer creates a wave of brilliant color when mass planted. Or use it as a background anchor to your garden, a wall or corner accent, or near a window, so you can enjoy all the action.

Highly attractive to butterflies, bees, hummingbirds, and many other insect pollinators; larval host for monarch (Danaus plexippus) and queen (D. gilippus) butterflies.

Colorado Blue Columbine

Scientific Name *Aquilegia coerulea*

Family Buttercup (Ranunculaceae)

Plant Characteristics Bushy, clump-forming, herbaceous perennial 1–2 feet tall and wide; compound leaves have numerous fan-shaped leaflets; masses of showy, 3-inch-wide, blue-and-white bicolored flowers have wide-spreading sepals and long, backward-pointing spurs that contain the nectar glands. Deer, rabbit resistant.

USDA Hardiness Zones 3a–7b

Bloom Period April–May

Growing Conditions Moderate sun to part shade; rich, moist, well-draining soils.

Adapted to a broad range of habitats from montane to subalpine forests and meadows, this state flower of Colorado has a variety of richly colored cultivars in the nursery trade. Tipped with exotic-looking flowers, the numerous stems rise above rounded clumps of fern-like basal leaves. The textured leaves and gorgeous flowers create a show-stopper accent for garden foregrounds, borders, entryways, and containers. Deadhead the spent flowers to encourage additional flowering. When the leaves fade, trim to the ground.

Attracts hummingbirds, butterflies, and bumblebees.

Colorado (Pingue) Rubberweed

Scientific Name *Hymenoxys richardsonii*

Family Aster (Asteraceae)

Plant Characteristics Herbaceous perennial 10–18 inches tall with multiple stems; leaves divided into narrow, thread-like segments; flowers clustered with 1–5 heads, each 1 inch wide with 8–14 bright-yellow rays surrounding yellow disk. Latex sap toxic to herbivores.

USDA Hardiness Zones 4a–7b

Bloom Period Summer (May–September)

Growing Conditions Full sun to part shade; coarse, well-draining soils, drought tolerant.

Pollinators flock to the nectar/pollen-rich flowers of this drought-tolerant, clump-forming wildflower. Native to pine forest openings, edges and understories, grasslands, and sage shrublands, it fits many garden micro-habitats. Mounds or ornate, thread-like leaves topped with arrays of bright-yellow flower heads create a color focus for garden foregrounds, walkway borders, mixed plantings, or in naturalized meadows. It colorscapes beautifully with blazingstar (blue), sticky geranium, and blanket flower (red-yellow). Also called Richardson's bitterweed.

Attracts butterflies, bees, and other insect pollinators.

Common Sunflower

Scientific Name *Helianthus annuus*

Family Aster (Asteraceae)

Plant Characteristics Annual with stout, branching stem 3–10 feet tall; leaves large, rough, heart-shaped; flower head 3–6 inches wide with yellow rays, brown disk. Deer resistant.

USDA Hardiness Zones 2a–11a; seeds cold hardy.

Bloom Period Summer (June–August)

Growing Conditions Full sun; coarse, well-draining soil; water 1x/month.

If the birds and bees formed a committee, they might vote the annual sunflower, with its full-service nectar bar and pollen buffet, as their favorite flower. Sunflowers create their own mini-ecosystem with nectar and pollen for a wide spectrum of pollinators, seeds for birds, and foliage for caterpillars. Small native bees to large bumblebees sip the nectar and provision their nests with pollen, while caterpillars dine on the leaves. Goldfinches and other seed-eating birds feast on the dried flower heads. Dozens of cultivars exist in shades of red and orange, from 2-foot dwarfs to 15-foot giants with 12-inch flower heads. So, really, find a place for this pollinator "supermarket." Plant a wildscape "forest" of 5–10 along a back wall or neglected space, or place 1–2 as a garden background accent. Multicolored dwarf cultivars make an attractive border, window planter, or patio container plant. More sun and water make bigger plants with more flowers. Sunflowers self-sow but are easy to control in a garden.

Attracts butterflies, bees, and many other insect pollinators, as well as hummingbirds and seed-eating birds, especially lesser goldfinches; larval host for up to 37 butterfly and moth species.

Common Yarrow

Scientific Name *Achillea millefolium*

Family Aster (Asteraceae)

Plant Characteristics Upright herbaceous, clump-forming perennial with 1–3-foot-tall flower stems; fern-like leaves grow in dense basal rosettes and on stems; flat-topped clusters of small white flowers bloom on stem tips. Deer and rabbit resistant.

USDA Hardiness Zones 4a–9b

Bloom Period Spring–summer (April–July)

Growing Conditions Prefers full sun, tolerates part shade; needs sandy, loamy, well-draining soil.

With delicate, lacy leaves and numerous flower stalks topped with showy 2–4-inch-wide clusters, this durable plant starts blooming early and lasts well into the summer. An eye-catching clump with a dozen bloom stalks adds foreground or mid-range color to gardens, landscape islands, and understory plantings for trees and shrubs. Extremely versatile, yarrow grows from deserts to alpine meadows, making most varieties in nurseries xeriscape hardy. White, yellow, and red cultivars and crosses are available, so mix and match for a vivid colorscape. The long-lasting flowers are good in floral arrangements. Deadhead the spent flower stems to prolong blooming. Yarrow is rhizomatous and can be aggressive in garden soils.

Attracts butterflies, bees, native flies, and other insect pollinators.

Cutleaf Anemone

Scientific Name *Anemone multifida*

Family Buttercup (Ranunculaceae)

Plant Characteristics Herbaceous, long-stemmed perennial 4–27 inches tall; basal leaves palmately with slender lobes, hairless to densely silky-hairy, depending on variety; flowers ½ inch wide with showy red-to-purple, yellow, or white sepals. Deer, rabbit resistant.

USDA Hardiness Zones 3b–8b

Bloom Period Spring–summer (March–July)

Growing Conditions Full sun to part shade; coarse, moist, well-draining soils.

Native to seasonally moist soils in open forests, slopes, and meadows, red windflower, or cutleaf anemone, grows from the foothills to alpine meadows. In the garden, the clumps of 10–15 stems add a dramatic, early-spring accent to foregrounds, borders, rock gardens, or window boxes. The circle of petals focuses the sun onto the stamens to hasten pollen maturity and provides a heated shelter for bees to warm up on chilly days. This adaptable perennial has many varieties and cultivars, including ones with intense red flowers and white flowers. If not available potted, sow seeds directly into moist soil or starter pots in the fall or early spring. Clumps can be divided. For best results, because of its variability and many varieties, choose locally sourced plants or seeds.

Provides important early spring pollen and nectar for bees, moths, and other insect pollinators.

Desert Prince's Plume

Scientific Name *Stanleya pinnata*

Family Mustard (Brassicaceae)

Plant Characteristics Herbaceous perennial, branching from base with multiple erect, slender stems 1–4 feet tall; leaves narrow, lance-shaped, lobed or not; flower clusters long, bottlebrush-like plumes on stem tips, flowers yellow, tubular with 4 spreading petal lobes and long extended stamens; slender seed pods form below flowers as bloom proceeds up the stem. Deer, rabbit resistant.

USDA Hardiness Zones 4a–9a

Bloom Period Spring–summer (April–September)

Growing Conditions Full sun; coarse, well-draining soils, heat and drought tolerant.

Native to open washes and canyons in arid sage shrub and grasslands to pinyon-juniper foothills, desert prince's plume is the perfect candidate for dry, hot, mid-elevation garden spots with sandy, rocky soil. Decorative 6-inch-long plumes of lemon-yellow flowers line the tall stems, and as the month-long blooming season progresses, long, slender seed pods dangle below the spent flowers. Use this arid land plant as a background color accent, a wall border, for xeriscape plantings, and in open naturalized and wildscapes. For colorscaping, it's compatible with Rocky Mountain beeplant, gayfeather, scarlet globemallow, and prairie-clovers. If potted plants are not available, it's easy to start from seeds; sow anytime.

*Attracts butterflies, bees, bumblebees, and many other insect pollinators; larval host for Becker's white (*Pontia beckerii*) and western white (*P. occidentalis*) butterflies.*

Dwarf Larkspur

Scientific Name *Delphinium nuttallianum*

Family Buttercup (Ranunculaceae)

Plant Characteristics Upright herbaceous perennial 1–2 feet tall; rounded leaves with deep, narrow lobes mainly on the lower ¼ of stem; flowers have 5 showy blue-to-purple, petal-like sepals with a distinctive spur in the rear and grow in terminal spikes on the stem tips. Deer, rabbit resistant.

USDA Hardiness Zones 6a–9a

Bloom Period Spring–summer (March–July)

Growing Conditions Performs best in full sun, tolerates part shade; needs natural, well-draining soil.

Native to mid-elevation, dry meadows, and opening areas from sage scrub to ponderosa forests, this early-blooming, colony-forming larkspur thrives in pollinator gardens. Once it finds a happy home, it won't be alone for long. Leave the dried stalks to self-seed, and your garden will greet the following spring with waves of purples and blues, as well as a host of hungry bees. As many as 15 spurred flowers bloom from the bottom up on each stalk. A weekly drink prolongs blooming. Also called meadow, Nuttall's, two-lobe, and low larkspur. Sow delphinium seeds in the fall so overwintering will break cold dormancy.

Attracts bees, butterflies, and hummingbirds.

Fireweed

Scientific Name *Chamerion angustifolium*

Family Evening Primrose (Onagraceae)

Plant Characteristics Herbaceous perennial 2–6 feet tall with leafy stems, forms dense colonies; leaves lance-shaped, to 9 inches long; flowers deep pink, 1½ inches wide with 4 spreading petals, blooms in dense, 20-inch-long spikes on stem tips. Not deer, rabbit resistant.

USDA Hardiness Zones 5a–10a

Bloom Period Summer (June–September)

Growing Conditions Full sun; rich, well-draining soils; occasional water helps produce vigorous growth, flowering.

Famous for blanketing open hillsides, especially after fires, with waves of pink blooms, these robust flowers with towering stems are perfect for a mass planting in a flower box, background screen, or naturalized area. Flowers open from the bottom of the spike upward, so pollinators have a summer-long source of pollen and nectar. Spreads by rhizomes to form dramatic stands but can become unruly in rich garden soil. Slender pods mature in late summer with fluffy seeds, resulting in the expression, "When fireweed goes to cotton, summer is forgotten." Leaves turn brilliant orange in fall.

Major nectar and pollen source for all pollinators; highly attractive to hummingbirds; likely larval host for 15 butterfly and moth species.

Gayfeather

Scientific Name *Liatris punctata*

Family Aster (Asteraceae)

Plant Characteristics Upright herbaceous perennial 1–2 feet tall and wide with multiple stems; leaves are narrow, grass-like, crowded near the base, smaller up the stem; small, pinkish-purple flowers with showy stamens are packed in narrow spikes reaching 10 inches long along the stem tips. Deer and rabbit resistant.

USDA Hardiness Zones 4a–9b

Bloom Period Summer–fall (August–October)

Growing Conditions Full sun, tolerates dappled shade; natural, coarse, well-draining soil.

In late summer when grasses turn dormant brown and many flowers fade, gayfeather, also called blazing star, comes into its glory. Slender, leafy stems blaze with long spikes of showy flowers that bloom from the top down. The fall buffet of pollen and nectar provides an important food source for a host of bees and butterflies before winter arrives. The vertical flower stems make a colorful border or foreground in a garden, or an eye-catching fill-in plant between shrubs. In a mixed planting, purple gayfeather complements the yellow fall blooms of goldenrods, snakeweed, and blanket flower. Gayfeathers spread by root corms to form large clumps and freely self-seed to form colonies. A deep drink twice a month during the summer will increase fall blooming.

Attracts butterflies, bees, and many other insect pollinators and hummingbirds.

Golden Columbine

Scientific Name *Aquilegia chrysantha*

Family Buttercup (Ranunculaceae)

Plant Characteristics Clump-forming herbaceous perennial 1–3 feet tall and wide; compound leaves have numerous fan-shaped leaflets; masses of showy, 3-inch-long yellow flowers have wide-spreading sepals and long, backward-pointing spurs that contain the nectar glands.

USDA Hardiness Zones 3b–9b

Bloom Period Spring–summer (April–September)

Growing Conditions Full sun to part shade, especially in the afternoon; needs sandy-to-loamy, somewhat moist, well-drained soil.

Bushy with masses of spectacular, long-lasting flowers, and dense, ornamental foliage, golden columbine creates an eye-catching mass planting in a landscape island or along a border, wall, or fence. Use it as a dramatic patio accent, in a window box, or entry garden. Native to moist canyons, it can be overly stressed in hot, dry, sunny locations, so at lower elevations it may require protected exposures and a regular summer water drip. For a three-season habitat colorscape, mix it with blanket flower, wild bergamot, or black-eyed Susan, all with similar water requirements. Allow it to go to seed and it will form a long-lived colony. Nurseries offer varieties and cultivars of golden columbine selected for a range of plant and flower sizes.

Attracts hummingbirds, butterflies, bumblebees, and many other insect pollinators.

Golden Crownbeard

Scientific Name *Verbesina encelioides*

Family Aster (Asteraceae)

Plant Characteristics Upright annual with multiple stems reaching 1–4 feet tall and wide; hairy, gray-green leaves are triangular to lance-shaped; 2-inch-wide flower heads have 8–15 bright-yellow, 3-toothed rays around a yellow disk, and grow singly on elongated stalks. Deer, rabbit resistant.

USDA Hardiness Zones 5a–8b

Bloom Period Spring–fall (April–October)

Growing Conditions Performs best in full sun and natural, well-draining soil.

This quick-growing, aggressive rock star stakes it fame in mixed plantings, along borders and walls, and as a late-season colorscape accent. You can trim it back or let it become bushy with dozens of showy flowers. It provides a rich buffet of pollen and nectar through the summer, but especially from fall until first frost when it's most needed by bees and butterflies. Naturally growing in low- to mid-elevation, open, dry, disturbed areas, it thrives in garden settings and naturalized and wildscape areas with no supplemental water. Deadhead it to prolong dense blooming or if you don't want the prolific self-seeder to spread, but then again, birds find the seeds an important food. As nature's supermarket, this robust plant creates its own mini-ecosystem in your garden. Sow seeds in the fall. Also commonly called cowpen daisy.

Highly attractive to butterflies, bees, and many other insect pollinators; larval host for the bordered patch butterfly (Chlosyne lacinia).

Greenthread

Scientific Name *Thelesperma filifolium*

Family Aster (Asteraceae)

Plant Characteristics Clump-forming annual to short-lived perennial with multiple delicate stems 1–2 feet tall; crowded green leaves have thin, thread-like segments; flower heads 1½-inches wide with 8 yellow, notched rays around a yellow or reddish-brown disk. Deer and rabbit resistant.

USDA Hardiness Zones 5a–9a

Bloom Period May–September

Growing Conditions Full sun; rocky, sandy, well-draining soils; heat, drought tolerant.

Native from dry prairies and sage scrublands to foothills and ponderosa forests, this prolific bloomer comes with a deep cultural heritage. Indigenous Peoples used it as a tea, a dye, and as medicine. With a months-long bloom period, it will be a favorite staple of bees and butterflies in your garden. Use it as a colorful addition to a mixed border or a rock garden accent. It thrives in open, dry, disturbed soils, so it will be right at home in a xeriscape or naturalized meadow. Its airy foliage, bright-yellow flower heads, and habitat requirements pair well with white and purple prairie-clovers, groundplum milkvetch, and scarlet globemallow. It readily self-seeds, or you can sow seeds directly into soil in the fall. It's also called Indian tea and cota, along with several other thread-leaved species of *Thelesperma* that grow in the Rockies.

Highly attractive to butterflies, bees, and many other insect pollinators.

Groundplum Milkvetch

Scientific Name *Astragalus crassicarpus*

Family Legume (Fabaceae)

Plant Characteristics Taprooted, mounding herbaceous perennial 1–2 feet tall and wide; leaves pinnately compound with 4–16 pairs of elliptical leaflets; flowers purple, pink, creamy to white, 1 inch long on dense spike; pods fleshy, thick walled, dark red to purple, usually lying on the ground. Deer, rabbit resistant.

USDA Hardiness Zones 3b–6b

Bloom Period Spring (April–June)

Growing Conditions Full sun; dry, well-draining soils; water 1–2 times while growing to enhance flowers and fruit.

Think wildscape for this sprawling mound of leaves covered with spikes of vivid flowers ranging from purple to white. The branches spread so the fruiting plant often is surrounded with ornate, red, plum-like pods. Use for early-spring foreground color in an oval garden, border, or naturalized area. Native to prairies and foothills and drought-tolerant, groundplum milkvetch dies back to its deep taproot as summer progresses, but it returns the next year and readily reseeds.

Attracts bees, butterflies, and other insect pollinators; fruit and seeds eaten by birds and small mammals.

Hairy False Goldenaster

Scientific Name *Heterotheca villosa*

Family Aster (Asteraceae)

Plant Characteristics Leafy, herbaceous perennial with upright-to-spreading, 1–2-foot-tall stems; gray-green leaves lance-shaped, covered with grayish-white hairs; flower heads 1–1½ inches wide with 10–25 narrow yellow rays around a small yellow disk. Deer, rabbit resistant.

USDA Hardiness Zones 5a–8b

Bloom Period June–September

Growing Conditions Performs best in full sun, tolerates part shade; needs natural, coarse, well-draining soil.

Clumping with multiple stems and covered with ornamental silvery-gray hairs, this early-summer bloomer bursts into color with open clusters of up to 16 bright-yellow flowers per stem. It adds a vivid color accent to rock and cacti gardens, and when mass planted or in mixed group plantings, the foliage can form a soft-textured wave of color. Use in pollinator islands, garden foregrounds, and borders. Drought tolerant and low maintenance, it loves full sun and dry, coarse-to-loamy soils. Hairy false goldenaster is widespread throughout the Rockies and adaptable to pollinator gardens from mid-elevation grasslands to mixed conifer forest zones. Sow seeds anytime; it self-seeds and spreads, but is not aggressive in garden settings.

Attracts butterflies, bees, and many other insect pollinators.

Harebell

Scientific Name *Campanula rotundifolia*

Family Bellflower (Campanulaceae)

Plant Characteristics Herbaceous, perennial clumps with 4–16-inch-tall stems; rounded basal leaves wither early, stem leaves narrow to 3 inches long; flowers with 5 blue-violet petals, bell-shaped, united at base, flaring at tips. Deer, rabbit resistant.

USDA Hardiness Zones 3a–6b

Bloom Period Summer–fall (June–October)

Growing Conditions Full sun to part shade; coarse, medium-moist, well-drained soils; water regularly to promote flowering.

Spreading by roots and self-seeding, harebells thrive in garden settings. Clumps of nodding, star-shaped, blue flowers make a delicate accent to rock gardens, woodland borders, garden foregrounds, and naturalized areas. Mass plant with cutleaf anemone, blue flax, violets, and self-heal for a meadow-like habitat. Deadhead to prolong flowering. Seeds need to overwinter, so sow in the fall.

Attracts butterflies, bees, and other insect pollinators, as well as hummingbirds.

Heartleaf Arnica

Scientific Name *Arnica cordifolia*

Family Aster (Asteraceae)

Plant Characteristics Herbaceous perennial with stems 6–28 inches tall, tipped with (usually) 1 showy flower head 3 inches wide with yellow rays and disk; leaves heart-shaped to oval, lined with coarse teeth. Browsed by deer.

USDA Hardiness Zones 5a–7b

Bloom Period Summer (May–July)

Growing Conditions Full sun to part shade; rich, well-draining soils; water 1–2x/month.

Native to dry, mixed conifer-aspen forests and meadows, this colony-forming flower will accent a garden foreground, border, or naturalized area with bursts of brilliant yellow flower heads. Though most seeds are formed asexually, the flowers still produce abundant pollen and nectar. Plants spread by rhizomes, so colonies spread several feet across and are long-lived. Occasional watering keeps the flowers vigorous. Of the dozen or so species and varieties of *Arnica* common to the Rockies, all have similar landscape applications.

Attracts bees and butterflies and other insect pollinators. Likely host plant for white-lined sphinx moth (Hyles lineata).

Hooked-spur Blue Violet

Scientific Name *Viola adunca*

Family Violet (Violaceae)

Plant Characteristics Herbaceous perennial, rhizomatous, clump-forming with several erect, 3–6-inch-tall, leafy stems; leaves oval to heart-shaped, toothed; flowers 1-inch wide, dark blue to violet with 5 spreading petals, 2 side petals bearded, lower 3 have whitish base with purple lines, lowest has ¼–½-inch-long spur with nectar glands. Deer, rabbit resistant.

USDA Hardiness Zones 4a–9b

Bloom Period Spring–summer (April–August)

Growing Conditions Full sun to part shade; well-draining, sandy, gravelly, seasonally moist soils.

Given regularly moist garden soil and some shade, violets thrive and spread to create petite color accents for beds and borders, naturalized areas, and groundcover fill-ins. Generally, bees attracted to the nectar within the spur pollinate the showy flowers, but that's only half the story. By summer, tiny bud-like flowers develop on the lower stems that never open but self-fertilize. They produce copious amounts of seeds that are then ejected up to 4 feet from the plant. Violets are one of the major host plants for the large fritillary family of butterflies (Nymphalidae). Also called western blue violet. The Canadian white violet, *V. canadensis,* in the same range and habitat, has similar landscape applications.

Attracts bees and butterflies; host plant for fritillary butterflies, including the critically endangered Zerene fritillary (Speyeria zerene).

Mountain Blue-eyed Grass

Scientific Name *Sisyrinchium montanum*

Family Iris (Iridaceae)

Plant Characteristics Herbaceous perennial, clumping with many stems reaching 20 inches tall; leaf blades narrow, grass-like, mostly basal from rhizome nodes; flowers purplish-blue, ¾ inch wide with yellow throat. Deer, rabbit resistant.

USDA Hardiness Zones 4a–7b

Bloom Period Spring–summer (April–July)

Growing Conditions Full sun, part shade; sand to clay, well-draining; summer water 2x/month once established.

Native from grasslands and foothills to subalpine forests, this top-rated garden flower is pollinated by native bees, hover flies (bee mimics), and beetles, all major players in a pollinator habitat. Blue-eyed grass adds a splash of color to a walkway border, garden foreground, sunny slope, or a container planting. Its vibrant flowers and dense mounds of basal leaves soften hardscape boulders and rock gardens. The hues of its deep-blue-to-purple flowers colorscape well with pearly everlasting, evening primroses, and Rocky Mountain phlox. It readily self-seeds, or sow in the fall. You also can divide the rhizomes, so it will brighten your garden spring after spring.

Attracts butterflies, bees, native flies, and other insect pollinators.

Mountain Golden Banner

Scientific Name *Thermopsis montana*

Family Legume (Fabaceae)

Plant Characteristics Herbaceous, rhizomatous, perennial with erect stems 8–30 inches tall; leaves palmately compound with 3 elliptic leaflets; elongated clusters 3–10 inches tall have 10–60, yellow lupine-type flowers; pods 2 inches long. Deer, rabbit resistant.

USDA Hardiness Zones 4a–9b

Bloom Period Summer (May–August)

Growing Conditions Full sun to part shade; sandy, gravelly, well-draining, seasonally moist soils; water 1x/week in dry locations.

Native from sage brushlands to cool, moist montane and subalpine forests, stands of this colony-forming flower spread blankets of brilliant yellow flowers across meadows, forest understories, and roadsides. Planted in your garden, they attract hordes of bumblebees, the preferred pollinator, plus bees and butterflies. Mass plant as a color accent for borders and backgrounds, or place dramatically in naturalized or colorscaped openings. Occasional summer water in hot exposures will help maintain prime flowering. Easy to grow from pots or seeds. Soak seeds in hot water (180° F) and plant in fall ¼–½ inch deep.

Highly attractive to bumblebees, bees, and butterflies.

Narrowleaf Bluebells

Scientific Name *Mertensia lanceolata*

Family Borage (Boraginaceae)

Plant Characteristics Herbaceous perennial with a deep taproot and multiple leafy steams 8–16 inches tall; leaves narrow, lance-shaped, without lateral veins; flowers tubular with bell-shaped, blue-to-violet petal lobes. Deer, rabbit resistant.

USDA Hardiness Zones 4a–6b

Bloom Period Spring–summer (April–August)

Growing Conditions Full sun to part shade; well-drained, seasonally moist soils.

Single to clump-forming with arching stems and dangling clusters of blue flowers, this is a standout in show gardens, borders, accents, or fill-ins for dappled shady spots. Native from plains and foothills to subalpine forests and meadows, this adaptable flower thrives in garden settings. Sunny, hot locations may require supplemental water. Also called prairie bluebells. Other bluebell species native to the Rocky Mountains have similar landscape applications.

Attracts butterflies, bees, bumblebees, and other insect pollinators; host for police-car moth (Gnophaela vermiculata) and other moth species.

Nettleleaf Giant Hyssop

Scientific Name *Agastache urticifolia*

Family Mint (Lamiaceae)

Plant Characteristics Upright, profusely branched, herbaceous perennial 1–5 feet tall; gray-green, aromatic leaves triangular, 2 inches long; flowers two-lipped, tubular, rose to purple or whitish in whorls on 6-inch-long spikes. Deer and rabbit resistant.

USDA Hardiness Zones 3a–9b

Bloom Period Summer (June–September)

Growing Conditions Performs best in full sun (short plants), tolerates partial shade (tall plants); needs regularly moist, well-draining soil.

With long terminal spikes packed with 1–2-inch long, nectar-rich flowers, this hardy mint is a cornucopia for bumblebees, bees, butterflies, and hummingbirds. The hundreds of long-blooming flowers keep the pollinators busy all summer. Low-maintenance, drought and heat tolerant, hyssop creates a densely bushy addition to a mixed planting, a massed border, or a garden background. It makes an attractive large-scale container accent on a patio. Though shrubby, this plant freezes to the ground but is root hardy. Various *Agastache* cultivars and hybrids are popular in nurseries, all with the dominant feature of show-stopping whorls of rose-pink flowers loved by pollinators. Extra water in parched sites aids performance.

A rich nectar source for hummingbirds, butterflies, bumblebees, and bees.

New Mexico Checkermallow

Scientific Name *Sidalcea neomexicana*

Family Mallow (Malvaceae)

Plant Characteristics Herbaceous perennial, rhizomatous with slender stems 1–3 feet tall; leaves palmately divided into 5–7 deeply cut lobes; flowers cluster along upper stem with 5 pink-to-rose-colored petals, stamen column protruding. Deer, rabbit resistant.

USDA Hardiness Zones 4a–8b

Bloom Period Spring–summer (April–September)

Growing Conditions Full sun to part shade; clay-to-loamy soils, 2x/week irrigation prolongs blooming.

Resembling miniature hollyhocks, these colony-forming flowers thrive in rich garden soil. Native to moist meadows and stream banks, they require regular moisture, so if you have a regularly irrigated garden spot, you can enjoy a wave of pink throughout the summer. Clusters of 1½-inch-wide flowers cover the stem tips and attract pollinators from bees to hummingbirds. Mass plant for maximum effect, or nurture a patch as a wall accent, garden backdrop, or focal point. For colorscaping and increased pollinator diversity, mix with other moisture-loving plants like goldenrod, orange sneezeweed, showy milkweed, and wild bergamot. Propagate by root division or sow seeds in the spring after last frost, or use starter pots. Also called New Mexico checkerbloom.

Attracts, butterflies, bees, bumblebees, hummingbirds; larval host for up to 6 butterfly species, including the common checkered-skipper (Pyrgus communis), *painted lady (*Vanessa cardui)*, and gray hairstreak (*Strymon melinus*).*

Orange Sneezeweed

Scientific Name *Hymenoxys hoopesii*

Family Aster (Asteraceae)

Plant Characteristics Herbaceous perennial with 1–4 stems reaching 3 feet tall, topped with branching clusters of 3-inch-wide flower heads with narrow, spreading-to-drooping, yellow-orange rays around a mounding, yellow disk; leaves lance-shaped, edges without teeth or lobes. Deer, rabbit resistant.

USDA Hardiness Zones 5b–7b

Bloom Period Summer (July–August)

Growing Conditions Full sun (cool locations) to part shade; well-drained, moderately moist soil.

With a month-long blooming season and flamboyant clusters with up to 12 golden flower heads, orange sneezeweed brings a brilliant summer attraction after the spring bloomers have faded. Use it as a garden background, mass plant along a wall or border, or create an oval garden or container accent. Native to mountain meadows and stream banks, it requires specific habitat requirements to thrive. Give it cool growing conditions and regular moisture and watch the insects zoom in all summer. Sow seeds anytime.

Highly attractive to butterflies, bees, and other insect pollinators.

Pearly Everlasting

Scientific Name *Anaphalis margaritacea*

Family Aster (Asteraceae)

Plant Characteristics Upright, clump-forming, herbaceous perennial 1–2 feet tall; slender leaves are covered with white-woolly hairs on undersides; male and female flowers on separate plants; flower heads a tight cluster of pearly-white, papery bracts surrounding tiny yellow disk flowers.

USDA Hardiness Zones 3a–7b

Bloom Period Summer (June–September)

Growing Conditions Grows well in full sun or dappled shade; needs natural, well-draining soil.

With mounds of silvery, gray-green leaves and dense clusters of striking white-and-yellow flowers, this easy-to-grow plant stakes its claim as a long-lasting flowering accent in a garden foreground, border garden, or a mixed understory planting. For a dramatic colorscape, pair with similar-sized, bright flowers like blanket flower, sticky germanium, wild bergamot, and fringed puccoon. It spreads by stolons and with optimum conditions can form colonies. The flowers make attractive cut flowers, but leave some as important late-season nectar and pollen sources for pollinators.

*Attracts butterflies, moths, bees, and other insect pollinators; larval host plant for American lady (*Vanessa virginiensis*) and painted lady (*Vanessa cardui*) butterflies.*

Prairie Coneflower

Scientific Name *Ratibida columnifera*

Family Aster (Asteraceae)

Plant Characteristics Erect herbaceous perennial 1–3 feet tall; large leaves are deeply cleft into narrow lobes along the midrib; flower heads have 4–10 drooping rays that can be solid yellow, solid reddish-brown, or reddish-brown towards the center with yellow tips; the cone is brown and 2 inches long. Deer browse the leaves.

USDA Hardiness Zones 4a–9b

Bloom Period Summer (June–September)

Growing Conditions Performs best in full sun and loamy, coarse, well-drained soil.

One color isn't enough for this plant. Long flower stalks grow from robust stems and bear flower heads with rays either solid or bicolored with yellow and maroon. Growth starts in mid-spring, so the flowers mature and bloom all summer just when many spring flowers are fading and late summer-fall flowers are sprouting. The tall stems and ornate flowers will add an eye-catching accent in a corner or oval garden, or as a back-garden screen. Mass plant when possible in a pollinator island, sunny border, or naturalized area. This adaptable plant thrives in dry, loamy-to-sandy-gravelly soils and full sun, but a weekly deep watering in dry summers will keep it in prime condition. Easily grown from seed: when sown in spring, blooms the second year. Divide or thin the clumps every few years to maintain vigor. Dwarf cultivars are available. Also called Mexican hat and long-headed coneflower.

Attracts butterflies, bees, and many other insect pollinators.

Prairie Spiderwort

Scientific Name *Tradescantia occidentalis*

Family Spiderwort (Commelinaceae)

Plant Characteristics Upright herbaceous perennial 1–2 feet tall; leaves are long, narrow blades that sheath the stem; flowers have 3 blue-to-magenta, oval petals and blue filaments with contrasting yellow anthers; 1–3 flowers open in the morning on stem tips and wilt by afternoon, but new buds open every day; long, slender, blade-like bracts spread beneath each cluster. Deer, rabbit resistant.

USDA Hardiness Zones 4a–9b

Bloom Period Spring–summer (April–September)

Growing Conditions Performs well in full sun and partial shade; sandy, loamy, coarse, well-draining soil.

With showy 1–2-inch-wide flowers that fade in afternoon heat and slender, blade-like leaves, this attractive plant adds an understated accent to gardens. Every morning new flowers from the cluster of buds on the stem tips greet the day's foraging bees and butterflies. With up to 10 buds per cluster on each branch tip, the daily renewal extends the bloom period into several weeks. In nature, drought-tolerant spiderworts grow from dry prairies to ponderosa forests. In hot, low-humidity garden areas, it thrives in dappled shade with weekly supplemental water. Once established, spiderwort spreads by self-seeding and rhizomes, or you can divide the clumps. The seeds need cold conditioning, so sow in the fall. Also called western spiderwort.

Attracts butterflies, bees, and many other insect pollinators.

Purple Aster

Scientific Name *Dieteria canescens*

Family Aster (Asteraceae)

Plant Characteristics Upright herbaceous annual to perennial with branching stems 1–3 feet tall; green leaves are linear and toothed; numerous flower heads bloom in open clusters with bright purple-to-blue rays around a yellow disk; seeds have fluffy plumes.

USDA Hardiness Zones 4a–10b

Bloom Period Summer–fall (May–October)

Growing Conditions Performs best in full sun, tolerates dappled shade; needs well-draining soils.

This unappreciated-but-beautiful wildflower self-seeds and spreads so much that many consider it a weed, but don't be biased. These hardy, heat- and drought-tolerant flowers thrive in a variety of soil types, habitats, and disturbed areas, so they will brighten up bleak spots that resist your gardening efforts. The profusion of intense blue, 1–2-inch-wide flowers start blooming in early to midsummer and don't stop until first frost. The long bloom period is a boon for bees and butterflies, especially in the fall. Purple asters aren't very tidy looking, but they're a good addition to mixed plantings, wildscape and xeriscape areas, or wherever the windborne seeds happen to volunteer. Also called hoary tansyaster.

*Highly attractive to butterflies, bees, and many other insect pollinators; larval host plants for sagebrush checkerspot (*Chlosyne acastus*), pearl crescent (*Phyciodes tharos*), and field crescent (*P. pulchella*) butterflies.*

Purple Locoweed

Scientific Name *Oxytropis lambertii*

Family Legume (Fabaceae)

Plant Characteristics Herbaceous rhizomatous perennial with multiple 4–16-inch-tall flower stems from base; basal leaves pinnately compound, 8 inches long with 9–19 oblong leaflets with silvery hairs; spikes erect, 2–4 inches long, crowded with magenta-to-pink or light-blue flowers; pods cylindrical. Deer, rabbit resistant.

USDA Hardiness Zones 3a–8b

Bloom Period Spring–summer (April–August)

Growing Conditions Full sun; coarse, well-draining soil, drought tolerant.

Native from grasslands and sage scrublands to foothills and pine montane forests, this hardy, adaptable plant adds a splash of brilliant color all summer long to a xeriscape habitat. Its clustered leafy stems supply a green foliage accent, while the spikes of brilliant flowers paint hot, dry, difficult natural spaces. For mass planting along walkway borders, in small color patches, or colorscaping, pair with white and purple prairie-clovers, scarlet globemallow, or gayfeather. Seeds need period of cold scarification, so sow directly in the ground in the fall, or refrigerate for 2 months for spring planting. Toxic to livestock. White locoweed, *O. sericea,* has similar habitat requirements and landscape applications.

Attracts bees, bumblebees (the primary pollinators), as well as butterflies, beetles, and hummingbirds; larval host for Queen Alexandra's sulfur butterfly (*Colias alexandra*), and other butterfly and moth species.

Purple Prairie-clover

Scientific Name *Dalea purpurea*

Family Legume (Fabaceae)

Plant Characteristics Upright herbaceous perennial 1–3 feet tall; compound leaves have 3–5 narrow, linear leaflets; small purple flowers grow in a ring around dense, hairy, cylindrical spike 1–2 inches long on the tips of tall, erect stems. Deer, rabbit resistant.

USDA Hardiness Zones 4a–8b

Bloom Period Spring (May–September)

Growing Conditions Requires full sun; sandy, loamy, well-draining soil.

Tall flower stalks tipped with spikes of delicate flowers wave above a vase-shaped mound of leafy stems. The small flowers have purple petals with golden anthers and bloom in a ring that progresses up the cylindrical spike. The long bloom period provides a month-long nectar-and-pollen buffet for bees and butterflies. Mass plant with white prairie-clover for a colorscape that's irresistible to an amazing variety of pollinators. For added diversity, include compatible plants such as sunflowers, blazingstar, and yellow beeplant. Purple prairie-clover is striking as a border plant, a mid-garden wave of color, and an accent in wildscaped areas. Native to grasslands and foothills, it's drought tolerant with a deep taproot, but a regular deep watering helps maintain prime condition.

Attracts a host of bees, butterflies, and many other insect pollinators; larval host for the southern dogface butterfly (Zerene cesonia).

Quamash

Scientific Name *Camassia quamash*

Family Asparagus (Asparagaceae)

Plant Characteristics Perennial from deep bulb, leaves basal, erect, grass-like to 20 inches long, 1 inch wide; dense spike-like clusters on stalk 8–28 inches tall, flowers blue, 2 inches wide, star-like. Deer, rabbit resistant.

USDA Hardiness Zones 4a–8b

Bloom Period Spring (April–May)

Growing Conditions Full sun, part shade; rich, soil, spring moisture, drier after flowering.

The Lewis and Clark expedition loved this plant. Quamash bulbs provided a major food source for the group, as well as the surrounding Native American tribes, so they bring a long botanical heritage to your habitat. Native from grasslands to montane forest meadows, quamash needs spring moisture while blooming, then a drier summer. It readily naturalizes by bulblets and self-seeding if left undisturbed, making it ideal for spectacular waves of color in mass plantings, borders, color accents in beds, and fill-ins under shrubs. Their early-spring blooming adds a splash of color before the summer perennials begin their show. The spikes bloom from the bottom up, extending the blooming season for the numerous insects that feast on the nectar-pollen-rich flowers. Bulbs are usually available in several varieties and colors. Plant in fall 4–6 inches deep, 6 inches apart. Also called blue quamash and Indian hyacinth; formerly classified in the lily family.

Highly attractive to butterflies, bees, bumblebees, beetles, and other insect pollinators.

Rocky Mountain Beeplant

Scientific Name *Peritoma serrulata*

Family Beeplant (Cleomaceae)

Plant Characteristics Herbaceous annual with 1–4-foot-tall, leafy, branching stems; leaves have 3 elliptic leaflets and grow up the stem into the flower cluster; elongated spikes on branch tips, flowers ½-inch long with 4 pink petals and long, showy purple stamens; slender fruit pods dangle down below the lower flowers. Deer, rabbit resistant.

USDA Hardiness Zones 3a–8b

Bloom Period Summer (June–August)

Growing Conditions Performs best in full sun, tolerates dappled shade; needs natural, coarse, well-drained soils.

A stand of this tall, branching plant will create a pink cloud of blooms with hordes of pollinators diving in and out. Aptly named, beeplant produces copious amounts of nectar and pollen for bees, butterflies, and hummingbirds. The hot-pink flower clusters bloom from the bottom up, so the bloom period lasts for several weeks. Then birds feast on the thousands of seeds that drop from the dangling pods. Of course, enough survive in the soil to reseed the colony for years to come. For greatest effect, mass plant as a backdrop behind low-growing flowers, as a wall border, corner or patio color accent, or in a wildscape or naturalized area. Also called Indian spinach, beeplant produces a yellow-green dye that the Navajo use for blankets and the black paint that Acoma potters use for the intricate designs on their pottery.

Highly attractive to bees, butterflies, hummingbirds, and many other insect pollinators; larval host for checkered, spring, western, Becker's, and checkered white butterflies (Pontia species).

Rocky Mountain Groundsel

Scientific Name *Packera streptanthifolia*

Family Aster (Asteraceae)

Plant Characteristics Herbaceous perennial with single-to-clustered flowering stems reaching 4–20 inches tall; basal leaves egg-shaped to elliptic, 1½ inches long, toothed; stem leaves few, smaller; flower heads in branching arrays on stem tips, 8 or 13 yellow rays, disk yellow. Deer, rabbit resistant.

USDA Hardiness Zones 4a–7b

Bloom Period Spring–fall (May–September)

Growing Conditions Full sun to part shade; dry-to-moist, coarse-to-loamy soils.

Widespread in open montane and subalpine forests, meadows, and slopes, this adaptable midsize flower is well suited for borders, garden foreground accents, and naturalized or wildscaped areas. Its showy clusters of bright-yellow flowers add long-lasting color and month-long nectar and pollen for pollinators. It spreads by rhizomes to form colonies, but not aggressively. You may have to seed this plant yourself, so sow fresh seeds in flats outdoors in the summer for same-summer or next-spring germination. Once established, it readily self-seeds.

Attracts butterflies, bees, bumblebees, native flies, and other insect pollinators; host plant for moth species.

Rocky Mountain Iris

Scientific Name *Iris missouriensis*

Family Iris (Iridaceae)

Plant Characteristics Herbaceous, perennial, rhizomatous, colony forming; leaves erect, blade-like, 18–24 inches long; flowers have erect blue petals and 3 spreading petal-like sepals purple to whitish with strong blue lines and a yellow base. Deer, rabbit resistant.

USDA Hardiness Zones 5a–7b

Bloom Period Summer (May–July)

Growing Conditions Full sun, tolerates partial shade, well-draining, seasonally moist soils, keep moist during flowering and for 6 weeks afterwards.

Mass planted in an oval garden, foreground, or border, this showy iris adds a formal look with its broad, sword-like iris leaves and classic ornamental flowers. Native to wet meadows, slopes, and seeps in montane to subalpine forests, it needs moist soil while blooming to perform at peak. For a mixed planting, choose other moisture-loving plants like self-heal, bunchberry, and violets. For quick color, plant rhizomes July–September, or sow seeds in the fall, but it takes several years to produce flowers. Divide rhizome clumps in the fall. Also called western blue flag iris.

Attracts butterflies, bees, native flies, as well as hummingbirds; likely host plant for 4 moth species.

Rocky Mountain Penstemon

Scientific Name *Penstemon strictus*

Family Plantain (Plantaginaceae)

Plant Characteristics Upright evergreen perennial with multiple flowering stems 1–3 feet tall; spreads by rhizomes; leaves narrow, pointed in basal clumps and paired on stems; blue-to-purple tubular flowers have 3 overhanging lower lobes as a landing pad for bees and 2 upper lobes that hood the anthers; flowers grow in pairs on one side of a crowded spike. Deer, rabbit resistant.

USDA Hardiness Zones 4a–9b

Bloom Period Summer (May–July)

Growing Conditions Performs best in full sun, tolerates dappled shade; needs natural, coarse, well-draining soils.

Easy to grow, this pollinator magnet readily self-seeds and spreads by rhizomes to form colonies from late spring through midsummer. Its blue color, large lower-lip landing pad, and inflated tubular shape are all specialized for bee pollination, but count on every butterfly, native fly, and passing hummingbird to join the feeding frenzy. Native to slopes, forests, and mountain meadows, this adaptable penstemon forms dense stands as a border or in a naturalized wildscape and adds a color accent to a mass planting along a wall or fence or a landscape oval. Deadhead to keep it tidy, but leave a few stems if you want it to spread by reseeding. Cultivars with various hues of blue and purple are available.

Highly attractive to bees, also hummingbirds, butterflies, and many other insect pollinators; likely host to 14 butterfly species, including checkerspot species and common buckeye (Junonia coenia).

Rocky Mountain Phlox

Scientific Name *Phlox multiflora*

Family Phlox (Polemoniaceae)

Plant Characteristics Herbaceous perennial, mound forming 6–18 inches wide, 6 inches high; leaves in bundles, narrow, pointed; flowers in crowded clusters, tubular with 5 flaring, white petal lobes. Deer, rabbit resistant.

USDA Hardiness Zones 3a–7b

Bloom Period Summer (June–August)

Growing Conditions Full sun; coarse, well-draining soils.

Native from grasslands and foothills to montane and subalpine forest openings and meadows, this adaptable plant will provide a small-scale, showy accent wherever planted. For a rock-garden specimen, nestle it against a colorful rock, or use as a garden foreground highlight, or add color to a rock-lined border. For colorscaping, mix with penstemons, yarrow, harebell, and other small-scale flowers with leafy basal mats. By summer a mass of fragrant flowers blankets the compact mound obscuring the leaves. Bumblebees and bees flock in for the nectar and pollen buffet. The similar longleaf phlox, *P. longifolia,* with white-to-pink flowers, has similar landscape applications.

Attracts bees, bumblebees, butterflies, and other insect pollinators.

Rydberg's Penstemon

Scientific Name *Penstemon rydbergii*

Family Plantain (Plantaginaceae)

Plant Characteristics Herbaceous perennial, clump-forming with multiple stems 8–24 inches tall; leaves lance-shaped to elliptic, in opposite pairs on stem; flowers in dense whorled clusters spaced around bare stalk, tubular, blue, violet, purple. Deer, rabbit resistant.

USDA Hardiness Zones 4a–7b

Bloom Period Summer (June–August)

Growing Conditions Full sun to part shade; well-draining soils, keep moist in summer.

Take it from the bees, a habitat garden can't have too many penstemons. The tubular shape of various species is designed for the size of the bees that pollinate it. Rydberg's flowers have a small diameter and attract small bees. Yet bumblebees, butterflies, and hummingbirds eagerly visit for nectar. The dense bundles of purple flowers are showstoppers in a garden, but they do like regularly moistened soil, especially during hot summers. Plant as stand-alone accents, or pair with columbines, blue flag iris, violets, and Jacob's ladder for borders, oval gardens, and colorscape mixes. Sow seeds in the fall, as they need winter temperatures to trigger spring germination.

*Highly attractive to small bees, bumblebees, butterflies, and other insect pollinators, as well as hummingbirds; likely host to 14 butterfly species, including Chalcedon checkerspot (*Euphydryas chalcedona*), arachne checkerspot (*Poladryas arachne*), and common buckeye (*Junonia coenia*).*

Scarlet Globemallow

Scientific Name *Sphaeralcea coccinea*

Family Mallow (Malvaceae)

Plant Characteristics Herbaceous perennial, rhizomatous, clump-forming with multiple stems 4–18 inches tall and wide; leaves palmate with 3–5 narrow, hairy lobes; flowers 1 inch wide, in dense, short clusters along branch ends, petals salmon, pink, red-orange, orange. Browsed by deer, rabbits.

USDA Hardiness Zones 6a–8b

Bloom Period Summer (May–July)

Growing Conditions Full sun; coarse, well-draining soils, heat and drought tolerant.

Native to openings and disturbed areas in grasslands, prairies, sage shrublands, and pinyon-juniper foothills, this hardy, low-maintenance survivor will thrive in and brighten difficult hot, dry garden areas. From spring through summer, brilliant orange-to-brick-red, cup-shaped flowers cover rounded mounds of gray-green leaves. The small profile and long blooming season make it ideal for garden foregrounds, borders, rock and xeriscape gardens, and wildscape and naturalized areas. It spreads by rhizomes and readily self-seeds, so it can form colorful mass plantings, and is often used as a groundcover. Globemallows are nectar-and-pollen cornucopias. Sow seeds in the fall, and divide rhizomes in the spring; prune to keep dense and to rejuvenate.

Highly attractive to bees, butterflies, beetles, and other insect pollinators; larval host for up to 6 butterfly species, including the painted lady (Vanessa cardui) *and gray hairstreak* (Strymon melinus); *birds and small mammals eat the seeds.*

Showy Fleabane

Scientific Name *Erigeron speciosus*

Family Aster (Asteraceae)

Plant Characteristics Herbaceous perennial 8–24 inches tall, leafy; leaves unlobed, surfaces mostly smooth, edges lined with tiny ciliate hairs, even-sized along stem; clusters of up to 20 showy, 2-inch-wide flower heads have 75–150 narrow purple-to-pink or white rays packed around a yellow disk. Deer, rabbit resistant.

USDA Hardiness Zones 4a–7b

Bloom Period Summer–fall (June–October)

Growing Conditions Full sun, tolerates part shade; dry-to-moist, coarse, well-draining soils, regular summer moisture for best appearance.

Abundant in montane and subalpine open forests and meadows, this long-blooming beauty keeps the pollinators coming back to your habitat garden from summer through early fall. In gardens, more rosettes spread year to year to form showy colonies. Use for mid-garden color, borders, or naturalized areas. For three-season colorscaping, pair with yarrow, heartleaf arnica, sticky geranium, black-eyed Susan, and penstemons. Its numerous flowers provide an important source of late-summer nectar for bees. Deadhead to prolong blooming. Prorogate by sowing seeds in winter or early spring, or by dividing emerging rosettes in the spring. All fleabanes are excellent for pollinator gardens, but this one has the largest, most colorful flower heads.

Attracts butterflies, bees, and other insect pollinators.

Showy Goldeneye

Scientific Name *Heliomeris multiflora*

Family Aster (Asteraceae)

Plant Characteristics Upright, clump-forming, herbaceous perennial 1–3 feet tall and wide with wide, reddish stems; leaves are lance-shaped; the numerous 1–2-inch-wide flower heads have showy yellow rays, often lighter near the tips, and a yellow disk. Deer, rabbit resistant.

USDA Hardiness Zones 4a–8b

Bloom Period Summer–fall (July–October)

Growing Conditions Performs best in full sun, tolerates dappled shade; needs coarse, well-draining soil.

Bushy and up to 3 feet tall and wide and with 25 or more brilliant flower heads per plant, showy goldeneye earns both its common and Latin names. Its moderate size, airy branching, and colorful flowers suit it well for informal plantings, borders, pollinator islands, and mixed-species meadow gardens. Its fall flowers add a splash of late-season color to gardens and provide a rich source of pollen and nectar when many plants have faded. It naturally grows from mid-elevation foothills to subalpine habitats in dry meadows, slopes, open woodlands, and roadsides, so it will be stressed at hotter, lower evaluations with scorching sun. It's easy to grow from seed, sow anytime, and it spreads by self-seeding. Horticultural cultivars are often available with color hue variations and shorter, more compact forms. Sow seeds in early spring.

Attracts butterflies, bees, and many other insect pollinators.

Showy Jacob's Ladder

Scientific Name *Polemonium pulcherrimum*

Family Phlox (Polemoniaceae)

Plant Characteristics Herbaceous, perennial, clump-forming 8–16 inches tall and wide; leaves pinnately compound with 11–25, oval-to-egg-shaped leaflets; flowers in dense clusters on branch tips, bell-shaped, blue or violet to whitish. Deer, rabbit resistant.

USDA Hardiness Zones 5a–7b

Bloom Period Summer (May–August)

Growing Conditions Full sun to part shade; moderately moist, well-draining soils.

With abundant summertime clusters of brilliant blue flowers with dainty yellow throats and long, feathery, ornate leaves, this plant earns its name "showy." It thrives in garden settings, adding years of beautiful color. Use it in dappled-shade gardens, woodland borders, foregrounds, or patio containers. For mixed colorscape plantings, pair it with cutleaf anemones, columbines, arnicas, and blanketflowers. Cultivars with green-and-yellow variegated leaves are available. Sow seeds in the fall. Tall Jacob's ladder *(P. caeruleum)* has similar landscape applications.

Attracts butterflies, bees, bumblebees, and many other insect pollinators.

Showy Milkweed

Scientific Name *Asclepias speciosa*

Family Dogbane (Apocynaceae)

Plant Characteristics Upright taprooted, herbaceous perennial 1½–3 feet tall; large blue-green, oval leaves with hairy undersides; star-shaped, pinkish-white flowers grow in dense spherical clusters 4–5 inches wide; fruit a large, pointed pod covered with warty bumps. The milky sap contains poisonous cardiac glycosides that caterpillars incorporate to make the adult butterflies poisonous to predators. Deer and rabbit resistant.

USDA Hardiness Zones 3a–9b

Bloom Period Spring–summer (May–September)

Growing Conditions Requires full sun and natural, well-draining soil.

Want monarch butterflies? Plant milkweeds. Showy milkweed earns its name with tall stems covered with large broad leaves and showy clusters of pinkish-white flowers, followed by horn-like pods that split open and release seeds with feathery tails. With a long taproot, this milkweed is moderately drought tolerant but needs extra water for the first year and weekly in arid areas. It tolerates a variety of soil types but needs full sun. Plant it with buckwheats, sunflowers, and penstemons, and you'll provide habitat for butterflies, hummingbirds, and large and small bees. Showy milkweed and other milkweed species are the most important food and host plants for monarch butterflies and critical for their survival.

*Highly attractive to butterflies, bees, and many other insect pollinators; larval host for monarch (*Danaus plexippus*) and queen (*D. gilippus*) butterflies.*

Sidebells Penstemon

Scientific Name *Penstemon secundiflorus*

Family Plantain (Plantaginaceae)

Plant Characteristics Herbaceous perennial, clump-forming with numerous stems; leaves narrow, oval to lance-shaped; flowers in dense spikes on one side of stalk, tubular with flaring petal lobes, pink to blue or violet. Deer, rabbit resistant.

USDA Hardiness Zones 4a–8b

Bloom Period Summer (May–July)

Growing Conditions Full sun; coarse, well-draining soils, drought tolerant.

Common to foothills and montane forests in the Front Range and Southern Rockies, this drought-tolerant penstemon is perfect for sunny low-water gardens, rock gardens, xeriscape plantings, and low-maintenance naturalized areas. Dense clusters with wands of showy blue-to-purple flowers are magnets for bees, their primary pollinators, as well as any other pollinators looking for a sip of nectar. The flowers bloom on one side of the stem, so bees save energy by moving straight up, not circling, the stem. If potted plants are not available, sow seed in fall so winter temperatures will trigger spring germination.

Attracts bees, bumblebees, butterflies, hummingbirds; likely host to 14 butterfly species, including checkerspot species and common buckeye (Junonia coenia).

Silvery Lupine

Scientific Name *Lupinus argenteus*

Family Legume (Fabaceae)

Plant Characteristics Herbaceous, clumping perennial 1–3 feet tall and wide; leaves palmate with 5–10 narrow leaflets, tops silvery-hairy; pea-type flowers blue to purple, on dense terminal spikes above leaves. Deer, rabbit resistant.

USDA Hardiness Zones 3a–7b

Bloom Period Spring–summer (April–July)

Growing Conditions Full sun to part shade; coarse, well-draining soils.

This highlight accent brings show-stopping color and mounding leafy texture to open areas, borders, backgrounds, and patio container plantings. The abundant erect, 6-inch-long spikes of dazzling flowers attract all types of bees and other pollinators. In a few years, it can aggressively colonize sunny, open naturalized areas. For colorscaping, mix with blanket flower, Colorado rubberweed, skyrocket, or showy goldeneye. Try to find potted plants since germinating seeds is difficult. Recommendations call for soaking seeds 24 hours in cold water and planting immediately in seed flats; mist regularly during the day and cover with plastic to maintain humidity. Once established, transplant to the garden. Seeds can also be sowed directly in the ground in the fall. Scarifying (scratching the hard surface with sandpaper) enhances water absorption and germination.

Highly attractive to bees, bumblebees, butterflies, and other insect pollinators.

Skyrocket Gilia

Scientific Name *Ipomopsis aggregata*

Family Phlox (Polemoniaceae)

Plant Characteristics Herbaceous biennials to short-lived perennials, stems erect to 3 feet tall, slender with short flowering branches; leaves deeply lobed with narrow segments; flowers bright red with mottled throat, trumpet-shaped with narrow, 1-inch-long tube and 5 flaring tips. Deer, rabbit resistant.

USDA Hardiness Zones 2a–7b

Bloom Period Summer (May–September)

Growing Conditions Full sun; coarse, well-drained soils.

With brilliant red, tubular flowers dangling in loose clusters from short side branches, this eye-catching flower blatantly advertises for hummingbirds. It is common to slopes and openings in montane and subalpine forests, so in your garden give it a sunny location, moderate water, and enjoy the action. For a pollinator buffet, pair it with wild bergamot, western red columbine, fireweed, and western wallflower. Sow seeds anytime. Also called scarlet gilia.

Attracts hummingbirds, as well as butterflies and other long-tongued pollinators.

Smooth Blue Aster

Scientific Name *Symphyotrichum laeve*

Family Aster (Asteraceae)

Plant Characteristics Upright herbaceous perennial with smooth, green 1–3-foot-tall stems; lance-shaped to oblong-pointed leaves clasp the stem and get smaller upward; dense clusters of flowers on the branch ends have many ½–1-inch-wide flower heads with lavender-to-blue-violet rays around a yellow disk that turns reddish with age. Deer, rabbit resistant.

USDA Hardiness Zones 4a–8b

Bloom Period Fall (August–October)

Growing Conditions Full sun, tolerates dappled shade; coarse, well-draining soil.

For vivid fall color in your garden, and a rich source of pollen and nectar, fall asters fill the bill. The blue-to-violet rays and yellow-to-reddish disk will energize a habitat landscape with the constant traffic of pollinators. The plants spread by rhizomes, but not aggressively, and they readily self-seed, so once established they will bloom until first frost. The intense blue colors blend well with goldenrods, sunflowers, and white heath aster. This aster occurs in the Rockies at mid-elevations from plains to ponderosa forests, so in hot, dry garden locations it will need regular supplemental water for prime performance. Sow seeds in the spring and cover lightly. If available, other closely related native blue asters have similar landscape applications.

Highly attractive to butterflies, bees, and many other insect pollinators; larval host plants for northern, tawny, field, painted, and pearl crescent butterflies (Phyciodes species).

Sticky Geranium

Scientific Name *Geranium viscosissimum*

Family Geramiun (Geraniaceae)

Plant Characteristics Herbaceous perennial, mound forming, 15–36 inches tall, covered with sticky glandular hairs; leaves mostly basal on long stalks, palmately compound; flowers 1 inch wide, pinkish-lavender to deep purple-magenta in open clusters near stem tips; seed capsules elongated like a crane's bill. Deer, rabbit resistant.

USDA Hardiness Zones 4a–9a

Bloom Period Summer (May–August)

Growing Conditions Full sun to part shade; well-drained, loamy-to-coarse soils.

Native from grasslands and plains to montane forest openings and meadows, this adaptable plant feels at home in a variety of garden settings. The small-but-numerous purple flowers bloom continuously from spring through summer to attract a diversity of pollinators, and birds enjoy the seeds. Then the leaves turn hues of red in the fall. Consider it for three-season color in the middle of the garden, in borders, under plantings, in naturalized areas, and even in planters and containers. Seed germination is low, so it's best to propagate by stem cuttings. With sticky glands, the plant is thought to be protocarnivorous, with the ability to digest small insects to absorb nitrogen. Sow seeds in fall. The widespread Richardson's geranium *(G. richardsonii)*, which is smaller with white flowers, and various mounding hybrids have similar uses.

Nectar and pollen source for butterflies, bees, beetles, native flies; likely host for up to 11 butterfly and moth species; birds eat the seeds.

Streambank Wild Hollyhock

Scientific Name *Iliamana rivularis*

Family Mallow (Malvaceae)

Plant Characteristics Herbaceous, leafy perennial with multiple stems, 3–6 feet tall by 4 feet wide; leaves large, palmately lobed, maple-like; flowers 2–3 inches wide, rose to white, in loose to dense, erect spikes. Not deer, rabbit resistant.

USDA Hardiness Zones 3a–8a

Bloom Period Summer (June–August)

Growing Conditions Full sun; deep, moist, well-drained soil; water 1–2x/week in hot locations.

With tall, leafy bloom stalks covered with dense arrays of flamboyant flowers, wild hollyhock shouts, "Look at me!" Bees, bumblebees, and butterflies certainly pay attention. As a midsize color-and-texture focal point, its stature suits it for backgrounds, borders, fence-line accents, and naturalized areas. For colorscaping, pair with wild bergamot, fireweed, goldenrod, and arrowleaf ragwort. Mass plant it for extra drama. Native to open forested and disturbed areas, it needs full sun as well as moist soil, a tricky combination in many gardens. Seeds require scarification, often by fire in nature, so it's best to find potted plants ready to go. Also called mountain hollyhock.

Attracts, bees, bumblebees, butterflies, and other insect pollinators.

Sulphur Flower Buckwheat

Scientific Name *Eriogonum umbellatum*

Family Buckwheat (Polygonaceae)

Plant Characteristics Low-growing, mat-forming, evergreen perennial 1–2 feet tall and wide; gray-green basal leaves are oval to linear, 1 inch long, and crowded together; small yellow-to-creamy flowers form rounded clusters 4 inches wide on umbrella-like branching stem tips, flower color fades to reddish-brown. Deer, rabbit resistant.

USDA Hardiness Zones 4a–8b

Bloom Period Spring–summer (April–September)

Growing Conditions Performs best in full sun to dappled shade; needs coarse, well-draining soil.

This widely adaptable buckwheat grows from mid-elevations to alpine meadows with varieties ranging from groundcovers with petite 3-inch-long flower stems to low-mounding clumps covered with robust 1–2-foot-tall stems. But regardless of size, the dense clusters of showy, lemon-yellow-to-creamy-white flowers will highlight any garden location. The low habit is ideal for borders and small spaces, flowering accents around rocks, or color companions with taller species such as penstemons, blazingstar, and wild bergamot. There are 41 listed varieties and cultivars. Flower color varies from bright yellow to various shades of yellow, white, and red. This buckwheat naturally favors cooler zones above 5,000 feet, so summer protection for harsh exposures and supplemental water may be required at lower elevations.

Highly attractive to butterflies, bees, and many other insect pollinators; larval host for lupine blue (Plebejus lupini) *and mormon metalmark* (Apodemia mormo) *butterflies.*

Three-nerved Goldenrod

Scientific Name *Solidago velutina*

Family Aster (Asteraceae)

Plant Characteristics Upright herbaceous perennial with 2–3-foot-tall stems; basal and stem leaves are linear-oblong, pointed, and get smaller up the stem; dense, club-shaped-to-pyramidal clusters have small flower heads, each with 3–5 short yellow rays around a yellow disk on stem tips; spreads by rhizomes. Deer, rabbit resistant.

USDA Hardiness Zones 4a–7b

Bloom Period Summer–fall (July–October)

Growing Conditions Performs best in full sun, tolerates dappled shade; coarse, well-draining, seasonally moist soils.

With multiple head-high stems topped with dense, pyramidal-to-wand-like clusters, each with up to 100 small flowers, these pollen powerhouses are one of the most important sources of fall pollinator food, especially for honeybees and migrating monarchs. The Xerces Society lists goldenrods, whose nectar is 33% sugar, in the "Top 100 Plants to Save Bees." In your garden, use them for backgrounds, color patches, or wall accents. For a glorious all-season cornucopia for bees and butterflies, combine goldenrod with spring-and-summer-blooming species like milkweeds, gayfeather, and buckwheats. Numerous species and cultivars exist, from 1 to 5 feet tall, so choose one that matches your design. Extra water promotes rigorous growth, but they spread by rhizomes and can become aggressive in garden soils. Also called velvety goldenrod.

Highly attractive to butterflies, bees, and many other insect pollinators; larval host plant for up to 39 species of butterflies and moths.

Tufted Evening Primrose

Scientific Name *Oenothera cespitosa*

Family Evening Primrose (Onagraceae)

Plant Characteristics Mounding stemless, herbaceous perennial 3–12 inches tall and 12–18 inches wide; basal leaves are lance-shaped to elliptic, usually lobed or toothed; 2–3-inch-wide flowers open near dusk and fade to pink the next day; the long floral tube emerges from the root crown with 4 large, showy, white petals; buds are erect. Deer, rabbit resistant.

USDA Hardiness Zones 4a–10b

Bloom Period Spring–summer (April–September)

Growing Conditions Performs best in full sun, tolerates dappled shade; needs natural, dry, well-draining soils.

This eye-catching accent greets the moon like most flowers welcome the sun. As dusk approaches, the flowers open wide to attract moths, especially the sphinx moth. The next morning, bees pollinate the lovely, delicate flowers. Each flower lasts one day, but plants are in bloom for about a month. The clumps enlarge by spreading roots and make ideal garden border plants and, in time, groundcovers. It adds texture and color to xeriscape and rock gardens and is essential for moon gardens. This flower appreciates dappled, afternoon shade in hot locations. Supplemental water several times a month. The annual white-stem evening primrose (*O. albicaulis*) is bushier to 20 inches tall. Susceptible to black flea beetles, which chew small holes in the leaves.

Attracts moths and bees, especially sphinx moths.

Western Red Columbine

Scientific Name *Aquilegia formosa*

Family Buttercup (Ranunculaceae)

Plant Characteristics Erect herbaceous perennial with multiple stems 2–3 feet tall and wide; compound leaves with 3 fan-shaped leaflets; flowers dangle with showy yellow stamens and red petals forming long spurs. Deer resistant.

USDA Hardiness Zones 7a–10a

Bloom Period Spring–fall (April–October)

Growing Conditions Full sun to part shade; moist, medium-draining soil; summer water 1x/month once established.

Protect this delicate plant from sunbaked, arid locations; give it regularly moistened-but-not-waterlogged soil and dappled afternoon light, then marvel at the abundant crimson flowers and fine-textured foliage. Like fairy lanterns, the dangling flowers seem to float on a cloud of light-green leaves. Hummingbirds feast on the nectar hidden in the flower's long spurs, along with butterflies and bumblebees. The mounding plants make a colorful background, a pretty filling in a patio or poolside container, or an accent for a dappled corner. Or use them in a mixed planting with other part-shade plants like sagebrush bluebells, violets, or blue flax. To prolong blooming, deadhead spent flowers, or leave them to self-sow in your garden.

Attracts hummingbirds, butterflies, bees, and other pollinators; larval host for up to 5 moth species.

Western Sweetvetch

Scientific Name *Hedysarum occidentale*

Family Legume (Fabaceae)

Plant Characteristics Herbaceous perennial, mounding, branching, 1–3 feet tall and wide; leaves pinnately compound with 9–21 oval-to-elliptic leaflets; pea-type flowers in erect-to-arching, spike-like clusters with 20–75 purple-to-pinkish, drooping blooms; fruit a chain of oval, disk-like pods. Deer, rabbit resistant.

USDA Hardiness Zones 4a–8a

Bloom Period Summer (June–August)

Growing Conditions Full sun; coarse, well-draining, seasonally moist soils.

Native to open forests, slopes, meadows, and roadsides at medium-to-high elevations, this large, leafy mounding plant can be blanketed with flashy arrays of brilliant magenta flowers. With a summer-long blooming season, it will color your habitat garden and thrill bees and bumblebees with a rich buffet of nectar and pollen. In the fall, ornate chains of disk-like seeds add visual interest, and food for game and songbirds. The mounding size fits borders, backgrounds, landscape islands, and open naturalized areas. For three-season colorscaping, plant with buckwheats and sticky geranium, or pair it with small shrubs like leadplant, shrubby cinquefoil, and Woods' rose.

Highly attractive to butterflies, bees, bumblebees, and other insect pollinators; birds eat the seeds.

Western Wallflower

Scientific Name *Erysimum capitatum*

Family Mustard (Brassicaceae)

Plant Characteristics Upright herbaceous biennial to short-lived perennial 1–3 feet tall; basal and stem leaves are narrow and linear to lance-shaped; 1-inch-wide flowers have 4 yellow-to-orange, oval petals and bloom in dense, rounded clusters on the branch tips; fruits are slender, vertical pods below the flowers.

USDA Hardiness Zones 4b–9b

Bloom Period Spring–summer (March–September)

Growing Conditions Performs best in full sun, tolerates dappled shade; needs natural, coarse, well-draining soil.

Named wallflower because a related European species grows by walls, this widespread flower boasts flamboyant clusters of reddish-orange or bright-yellow flowers. Butterflies and bees seem to dance around the nectar-and-pollen-rich flowers. As the seed pods mature and split open, birds join the feast. The plants live about 2–3 years but prolifically self-sow. Directly sow seeds in fall or spring. It's an ideal wide-spectrum attractor for a limited-size garden. Plant in a foreground, along a wall or border, or for fill-in color. Mass plant with blue flax, Rocky Mountain penstemon, black-eyed Susan, or showy fleabane. Native to medium-dry habitats, this adaptable selection thrives with little attention.

*Highly attractive to butterflies, bees, and many other insect pollinators. Mustards are larval host plants for various white species (*Pontia *and* Pieris*), orange-tip species (*Anthocharis*), and the desert marble butterfly (*Euchloe lotta*).*

Whipple's Penstemon

Scientific Name *Penstemon whippleanus*

Family Plantain (Plantaginaceae)

Plant Characteristics Herbaceous perennial, clump-forming with multiple erect stems 8–26 inches tall; leaves basal and on stems, elliptic to lance-shaped; flowers in separated clusters along the stem, glandular hairy, dark purple to blue. Deer, rabbit resistant.

USDA Hardiness Zones 3a–7b

Bloom Period Summer (July–August)

Growing Conditions Full sun to part shade; coarse, well-draining soils, water regularly until established.

The dense clusters of eye-catching dark-burgundy flowers make this clump-forming flower a favorite for mid-elevation gardens. Glandular hairs cover tubular flowers with an added texture accent. The inflated throat, bottom-petal landing pad, and nectar guidelines are calling cards for bumblebees, the designated pollinators. Whipple's penstemon makes a dramatic border or garden foreground, accent for a dappled shady area, or patio color accent. If potted plants are not available, sow seed in fall so winter temperatures will trigger spring germination. Also called dusky penstemon.

Highly attractive to bumblebees, hummingbirds, butterflies, and many other insect pollinators; likely host to 14 butterfly species, including checkerspot species and common buckeye (Junonia coenia).

White Heath Aster

Scientific Name *Symphyotrichum ericoides*

Family Aster (Asteraceae)

Plant Characteristics Upright herbaceous perennial 1–3 feet tall; linear leaves are only ⅛–¼ inch wide, lower leaves wither by blooming; ½-inch wide, daisy-like flowers have white rays and a yellow disk and bloom in dense, cylindrical arrays on branch ends. Deer, rabbit resistant when mature.

USDA Hardiness Zones 5a–10b

Bloom Period Summer–fall (July–October)

Growing Conditions Full sun, tolerates dappled shade; coarse, well-draining soils.

Just when many summer flowers are withering, this showy flower comes to life with dense, cylindrical clusters with 100 or more small white flowers on the branch tips. As an essential fall nectar-and-pollen source for all types of pollinators, it ranks alongside goldenrods and sunflowers in importance. It's ideal for stretching late-season color in your garden well into the fall. Native from prairies and foothills to ponderosa forests, heath aster is a good match for xeriscape gardens. Its small scale fits limited-space rock and oval gardens. It spreads by rhizomes and will colonize naturalized open areas with loose soil. Prostrate groundcovers and densely flowering cultivars are sometimes available. Sow seeds in the spring and cover lightly.

*Attracts butterflies, native bees and flies, and many other insect pollinators; larval host for various checkerspots (*Euphydryas *species) and northern, tawny, field, painted, and pearl crescent butterflies (*Phyciodes *species), as well as many moths.*

White Prairie-clover

Scientific Name *Dalea candida*

Family Legume (Fabaceae)

Plant Characteristics Upright herbaceous perennial forming clumps 1–2 feet tall and wide; leaves are pinnately compound with 5–7 narrow leaflets; small white flowers bloom in a ring around a dense cylindrical spike to 3 inches long at branch tips. Deer resistant.

USDA Hardiness Zones 3a–8b

Bloom Period Summer (May–September)

Growing Conditions Requires full sun; needs well-draining, dry-to-moderately moist soils.

This nitrogen-fixing legume will fertilize your garden while providing a rich source of pollen and nectar for hordes of insect pollinators. One 2-foot-high clump can have dozens of stalks tipped with spikes of small-but-showy flowers. These taprooted prairie plants self-seed, so volunteers will spread their beauty year to year. For a dramatic pollinator-friendly garden, landscape island, or border, mass plant with purple prairie-clover, blanket flower, wild bergamot, and goldenrods. After a summer-long buffet for insects, birds will feast on the seeds. Native to prairies and eastern mountain slopes and foothills, it's drought tolerant with a deep taproot, but a regular deep watering helps maintain prime condition.

Attracts bees, butterflies, and many other insect pollinators; larval host for the southern dogface butterfly (Zerene cesonia).

Wild Bergamot

Scientific Name *Monarda fistulosa*

Family Mint (Lamiaceae)

Plant Characteristics Herbaceous perennial, clump-forming, rhizomatous, 3–4 feet tall; leaves are lance-shaped, minty aromatic; two-lipped tubular flowers are lavender to pink and grow in dense, rounded clusters on stem tips. Deer, rabbit resistant.

USDA Hardiness Zones 3a–8b

Bloom Period Summer (June–August)

Growing Conditions Performs best in full sun, tolerates dappled shade; needs natural, dry-to-moist, well-draining soil.

Spreading by rhizomes, this clump-forming landscape favorite will increase pollinator diversity. Hummingbirds, butterflies, and bees all flock to the nectar-rich flowers. In moist soil, the clumps spread year to year, plus it reseeds readily. It's heat tolerant and naturally thrives in pinyon-juniper and mixed-conifer woodlands above 5,000 feet along drainages in sun to partial shade. In hot exposures, it appreciates filtered shade and regular irrigation. With a long bloom period, wild bergamot will be a major attraction for up to six weeks. Use this versatile plant in patio accent gardens, perennial borders, background plantings, and in mass-planted and naturalized areas. The tall stems and showy lavender flowers go well with the yellows of showy goldeneye, arrowleaf ragwort, coneflower, and black-eyed Susan. Deadhead the flowers to prolong blooming, but leave late-summer blooms if you want it to reseed. Seeds will germinate without overwintering, so you can sow in the spring. Intensely colored cultivars are available in nurseries and by seed.

Attracts hummingbirds, butterflies, bees, sphinx moths, and many other insect pollinators.

Yellow Beeplant

Scientific Name *Peritoma lutea*

Family Beeplant (Cleomaceae)

Plant Characteristics Herbaceous annual with erect 1 to several, sparsely branching stems 1–3 feet tall; leaves palmate with 5 lance-shaped leaflets, each 1–2 inches long; dense elongated clusters form on branch tips, flowers lemon yellow, petals 4, stamens long, extended; fruit are narrow pods on long stalks that droop beneath ongoing blooms. Deer, rabbit resistant.

USDA Hardiness Zones 5a–8b; grown as an annual in colder areas

Bloom Period Summer (May–August)

Growing Conditions Requires full sun; dry-to-seasonally moist, well-draining, coarse-to-fine soils.

Native to arid soils from sagebrush to pinyon-juniper foothills and ponderosa forests, this drought-tolerant annual can form thick stands as a seed bank builds in the soil. The plant provides colorful cover in parched areas and will accent a sunny wall or fence. Buds in the flower spikes open progressively upward, so each cluster blooms for several weeks. Flowering continues from spring until early autumn. The prolonged bloom attracts a long parade of butterflies, bees, beetles, and other pollinators, and birds eat the copious seeds that drop. More than 140 species of 32 bee genre have been recorded feeding on yellow beeplant. For a dynamite combo, mix with pink Rocky Mountain beeplant.

Important source of pollen and nectar for butterflies, bees, beetles, and other pollinators; larval host for checkered, spring, western, Becker's, and checkered white butterflies (Pontia species).

Creeping Barberry

Kinnikinnick, Bearberry

Vines & Groundcovers

Self-heal

Silver Sage Wormwood

Thicket Creeper

Bunchberry

Combine a vine and a trellis and what do you get? A hanging garden that will decorate a barren wall, add leafy texture to a fence, or accent a landscape island. Robust climbing vines can cover a pergola to create a shady patio shelter with a leafy network of limbs, and also provide shelter and nesting sites for birds. Delicate vines add an understated touch of beauty to rock gardens or container plantings. Vines are fast-growing; some are well-mannered, while others get a bit rowdy and try to take over. Most perform best with shady roots and sun-bathed foliage.

Western Virgin's Bower

Lanceleaf Stonecrop

Bunchberry

Scientific Name *Cornus canadensis*

Family Dogwood (Cornaceae)

Plant Characteristics Low-growing, deciduous. colony-forming perennial 4–10 inches tall; leaves broadly elliptic, whorled around stem; flowers on short stalk at stem tip, tiny flowers clustered in center of 4 showy, white, petal-like bracts; fruit a cluster of red drupes ⅜-inch diameter. Deer, rabbit resistant.

USDA Hardiness Zones 4a–6a

Bloom Period Summer (May–July)

Growing Conditions Part to full shade; moist woodland soils; cool summers.

This mid- to high-elevation plant of moist spruce-fir-aspen forests needs a specialized habitat with regular moisture, part shade, and cool summers with few days exceeding 90° F. If that fits your habitat garden, you can use bunchberry to form a dominate groundcover, understory filler, or as a garden foreground accent. The three-season attraction has creamy-white flowers in the spring, brilliant red berries through the summer, and red-to-burgundy leaves in the fall. For a little pollination drama, the flowers have an appendage that launches an explosive burst of pollen when triggered by a bee and blankets it with pollen.

Bees, butterflies, other pollinators; birds and small mammals consume the fruit; may serve as a larval host for the summer azure butterfly (Celastrina neglecta).

Creeping Barberry

Scientific Name *Berberis repens*

Family Barberry (Berberidaceae)

Plant Characteristics Evergreen, prostrate, subshrub with creeping woody stems to 1–2 foot high; leaves pinnately compound with 3–7 oval leaflets with wavy, spine-tipped edges, reddish in winter; dense 1–4-inch-long clusters have 25–50 yellow flowers each ¼ inch wide; fruit a 3/8-inch-long blue berry. Deer, rabbit resistant.

USDA Hardiness Zones 5b–7b

Bloom Period April–June

Growing Conditions Full sun to full shade; coarse, well-draining soil, not heat tolerant, water 1–2x/month in sunny exposures.

Native to open woods and ridges in ponderosa-oak and spruce-fir forests, this creeping groundcover contributes spring clusters of bright-yellow flowers for the bees, summer blue-purple fruit loved by birds, and evergreen leaves that turn shades of red and orange in the winter. It spreads by roots and can fill empty spaces under trees and shrubs, line garden and walkway borders, or add color to rock accents. For colorscaping, mix with other open woodland plants like yarrow, larkspurs, penstemons, and blue flax. Cultivars have been developed with enhanced ornamental leaf-and-fruit features. Also called creeping Oregon-grape.

Attracts butterflies, bees, and other insect pollinators; host for up to 5 moth species; birds eat the fruit.

Kinnikinnick, Bearberry

Scientific Name *Arctostaphylos uva-ursi*

Family Heath (Ericaceae)

Plant Characteristics Evergreen prostrate, mat-forming subshrub groundcover with densely leafy stems reaching 1 foot tall, 6 feet wide; leaves egg-shaped, 1 inch long, turn red in fall; few-flowered clusters have nodding, urn-shaped flowers, ¼–¾ inch long, white to pink; fruit a berry-like drupe, matures red. Deer, rabbit resistant.

USDA Hardiness Zones 2a–6b

Bloom Period Spring (April–June); fruit ripens August–September

Growing Conditions Full sun to part shade; moist-to-dry, coarse, well-draining, forest soils.

Kinnikinnick is for cool summer habitat gardens. Native to conifer forests, it will spread over dry, sandy, gravelly areas to form a dense carpet of evergreen leaves. With spring flowers to attract bumblebees and butterflies, summer red fruit for birds, and bright-burgundy leaves in the winter, this amazing plant provides four seasons of ornamental accent and wildlife appeal. Let it sprawl over a boulder or rock border, accent a rock garden, or spread as an understory plant in a naturalized area. It's drought tolerant but in hot summers a 1–2x/month deep watering will keep it in prime condition. Propagate by tip cuttings in the fall.

Attracts butterflies, bumblebees, hummingbirds; birds eat the fruit; host for up to 54 butterfly and moth species, including the brown elfin (Callophrys augustinus) and hoary elfin (Callophrys polios).

Lanceleaf Stonecrop

Scientific Name *Sedum lanceolatum*

Family Stonecrop (Crassulaceae)

Plant Characteristics Succulent perennial with clustered, erect stems 1–4 inches tall; dense rosettes and lance-shaped stem leaves thick blue-green to red; clusters dense, flat-topped ⅓–2 inches across with 3–25 small yellow flowers. Deer, rabbit resistant.

USDA Hardiness Zones 4a–9b

Bloom Period Summer–fall (May–September)

Growing Conditions Full sun; rocky outcrops, dry, gravelly, well-drained soil.

These petite succulents may look tender, but they're tough. The brilliant yellow, star-shaped flowers and succulent reddish-green rosettes look out of place in the desolate gravelly, rocky openings where they thrive from foothills to alpine areas. In your yard, they bring a colorful accent to rock gardens, dry exposed areas, tucked among rock borders, or dangling from a crevice in a rock wall or boulder. The delicate stems break easily, but no worries. Just stick the stem in loose soil and they're guaranteed to root and create a colorful groundcover. Potted plants are often available, and it grows easily from spring-sown seeds.

Attracts butterflies, bumblebees, bees, and other insect pollinators; larval host to 9 butterfly and moth species, including the variegated fritillary (Euptoieta claudia) and common buckeye (Junonia coenia).

Self-heal

Scientific Name *Prunella vulgaris*

Family Mint (Laminaceae)

Plant Characteristics Herbaceous perennial groundcover with spreading, rooting stems 3–16 inches high; leaves lance-shaped, 1–3 inches long; tubular flowers pink, purple, ¾ inch long, upper lip hooded, lower lip with 3 lobes, in stout terminal spikes. Deer resistant.

USDA Hardiness Zones 5a–9a

Bloom Period Summer (June–August)

Growing Conditions Full sun, part shade; damp, sandy-loamy, well-draining soil; likes summer moisture.

With a worldwide distribution, this little mint has been a popular edible and medicinal herb in many cultures for centuries. In your pollinator garden, it thrives in periodically moist soils, sun or partial shade. The Xerces Society lists 10 butterfly, moth, and bee genera that forage on the plant. It spreads by rooting stems; it is well suited as a groundcover, border or edge plant, garden accent, mowed eco-lawns, and living-roof plants. Its summer-long blooms keep the pollinators coming back and adds an understory floral interest to trimmed-up shrubs and small trees, walkways, and containers. If you can't find starter plants, sow in seed flats in the spring and gently press into the soil. It spreads aggressively and can be divided. Replant plugs 6–12 inches apart.

Attracts bees, butterflies, and many other pollinators; birds eat seeds.

Silver Sage Wormwood

Scientific Name *Artemisia ludoviciana*
Family Aster (Asteraceae)
Plant Characteristics Herbaceous perennial, rhizomatous with erect stems 1–3 feet tall; leaves linear to lance-shaped, 4 inches long, surfaces woolly white, felt-like, very aromatic; flower heads insignificant, clustered on branch tips, yellowish to creamy-white. Deer, rabbit resistant.
USDA Hardiness Zones 4a–8b
Bloom Period Summer–fall (July–October)
Growing Conditions Full sun; coarse, dry, well-draining soil.

Though wild pollinated, this attractive groundcover has a place in a habitat garden as a host plant for numerous butterflies and moths. Yet, like all sage species, its windborne pollen and can cause allergies in people sensitive to hay fever. Silver sage wormwood spreads by rhizomes and forms a thick mat of underground roots, good erosion control and stabilization, but it can be aggressive in garden soils. That said, its ornamental stems and leaves matted with silver woolly hairs create an attractive knee-high groundcover. It's suited for naturalized areas with poor soils and hot, dry exposures. Use it as a walkway border; wall or background accent; or in a colorscape mix with purple aster, silvery lupine, or gayfeather. Several less-aggressive cultivars are available with especially vibrant foliage. Also called white or silver sagebrush, Louisiana wormwood, and cudweed sagewort.

Host plant for up to 30 butterfly and moth species, including painted lady (Vanessa cardui) *and American lady* (Vanessa virginiensis) *butterflies.*

Thicket Creeper

Scientific Name *Parthenocissus vitacea*

Family Grape (Vitaceae)

Plant Characteristics Deciduous perennial vine with sprawling stems reaching 6–30 feet long with tendrils for climbing; leaves have 5 leaflets with coarse teeth, turn red in fall; branching clusters of small greenish flowers followed by black, inedible berries. Deer, rabbit resistant.

USDA Hardiness Zones 4b–8b

Bloom Period Summer (June–August)

Growing Conditions Full sun, tolerates partial shade; well-draining, coarse soil with periodic moisture.

Native to mid-elevations across the Rockies, this vigorous vine climbs high into trees and sprawls over bushes and boulders. In your habitat garden, it will provide nectar and pollen for bees, as well as food, shade, and shelter for birds. Robins and other songbirds feast on the small-but-abundant fruit, and the leafy network of branches provides protected nesting sites for finches, doves, and other small birds. Functionally, the densely leafy vine will blanket a trellis or fence to create a seasonal screen or drape a patio structure for summer shade. Train it over a pole or stump for a vertical accent, or let it sprawl across the ground in a shady, naturalized area, but keep it trimmed off trees and shrubs. It climbs by twining the tendrils around vegetation or by inserting them into cracks in bark or masonry. Don't let the vine grow on structures that need periodic painting. You can build a wire grid to direct the vine along walls. In the fall, the leaves turn brilliant hues of red and burgundy. Prune in the winter. Also commonly known as woodbine.

Attracts bees and other insect pollinators; larval host for up to 8 butterflies and moth species; provides food, shade, shelter for birds.

Western Virgin's Bower

Scientific Name *Clematis ligusticifolia*

Family Buttercup (Ranunculaceae)

Plant Characteristics Bushy perennial, herbaceous vine has stems reaching 15 feet long; leaves have 5–7 toothed or lobed leaflets with twining tendrils; 1-inch-wide, creamy-white flowers lack petals but have 4 showy white sepals and grow in 3–8-inch-wide arrays; seeds develop on female plants in dense, pompom-like clusters with long feathery tails. Deer, rabbit resistant.

USDA Hardiness Zones 5a–10b

Bloom Period Summer (July–September)

Growing Conditions Performs best in full sun, tolerates partial shade with reduced blooming; needs medium moisture and coarse, well-draining soil.

This fast growing, robust vine quickly spreads and claims its territory. With twining tendrils, it covers trellises, lattices, and fences, as well as sprawling as a groundcover. Its densely bushy stems provide wonderful nesting habitat for finches, doves, wrens, and other songbirds. Bees and butterflies flock to the flower clusters. With separate male and female plants, only the females produce the ornate silky seed clusters. Though shade tolerant, like most vines, the more sun it gets, the more it blooms. A deep taproot makes it extremely drought tolerant, yet sun and moisture are required for robust booming. The easiest way to propagate it is by transplanting the sprawling stems that take root. Clematis species like cool roots, so mulch in hot sunny locations.

Attracts butterflies, bees, and many other insect pollinators; larval host for up to 8 butterflies and moth species.

Switchgrass

Grasses

Indian Ricegrass

Alkali Sacaton

Many bunchgrasses have highly ornamental qualities and are ideally suited for borders, pattern plantings, garden backdrops, group mixes or mass plantings, corner fill-ins, or as stand-alone accents. Native grasses are quick growing, deep-rooted and drought-tolerant, and low maintenance with no need for fertilizers. Grasses provide food, shelter, and nesting sites. They build soil and prevent erosion. In early spring, rejuvenate bunchgrass by sheering clumps to near ground level. The Xerces Society recommends at least two clumps of native grass in a pollinator garden.

Purple Three-awn

Alkali Sacaton

Scientific Name *Sporobolus airoides*

Family Grass (Poaceae)

Plant Characteristics Robust, warm-season, perennial bunchgrass reaching 2–4 feet tall and wide; leaves silvery-green, narrow, folded, arching, 2 feet long, golden brown in winter; florets pinkish to gold in spreading pyramidal clusters on ends of erect 3-foot stems; seeds grain-like. Deer, rabbit resistant.

USDA Hardiness Zones 4a–9b

Bloom Period Summer (June–September)

Growing Conditions Full sun, tolerates part shade; coarse, well-draining, occasionally to regularly moist soils.

Dense clumps of arching leaves and fountain-like sprays of waving seed heads make this bunchgrass a dominant accent for borders, backgrounds, screens, or naturalized areas. The mounds of arching leaves provide year-round texture, and the airy clusters of reddish seed heads blaze when backlit by the sun. Native to grasslands, plateaus, and foothills, alkali sacaton is hardy in most garden settings to around 7,500 feet in elevation. It self-seeds and spreads with a dense, fibrous root system. Numerous cultivars have been selected for size and leaf color. Leave clumps intact through the winter to protect overwintering insects, then shear to the ground in early spring to remove thatch before new growth appears.

Provides nesting for bees, hibernation for butterfly and moth pupae, and seed for game and songbirds; larval host for the sandhill skipper butterfly (Polites sabuleti).

Indian Ricegrass

Scientific Name *Achnatherum hymenoides*

Family Grass (Poaceae)

Plant Characteristics Herbaceous perennial, cool-season bunchgrass 1–2 feet tall and wide; basal tuft and stem leaves are narrow, wiry; nondescript flowers grow in dense spikes and mature with nutritious seeds. Highly palatable to deer and rabbits.

USDA Hardiness Zones 4a–7b

Bloom Period Summer (July–September)

Growing Conditions Performs best in full sun; needs natural, sandy, coarse, well-draining soil.

Native from desert scrub to grasslands and ponderosa forests, this drought-tolerant bunchgrass starts the spring with a dense tuft of green leaves and soon develops ornate seed heads. By midsummer, the dormant leaves turn golden brown and the lacy seed heads dominate with clusters of zigzag branches tipped with nuggets of ivory-colored seeds. Small mammals feast on the nutritious seeds, butterflies and moths lay their eggs on the leaves, and bees use the dense basal clump as nesting and overwintering sites. As a small-scale garden accent, Indian ricegrass adds texture to borders, rock gardens, and mixed container plantings. Combines well with snakeweed, scarlet globemallow, and groundplum milkvetch. Thrives with 8–14 inches of annual rain, so in arid sites a few deep drinks in the spring will help it develop. Seed coat and embryo dormancies inhibit germination; seeds should be planted ½–1 inch deep in fine soils and 1–3 inches deep in coarse soils.

Provides seeds for birds and small mammals, nesting and overwinter habitat for bees; larval host for grass skipper butterfly species (Hesperiidae).

Purple Three-awn

Scientific Name *Aristida purpurea*

Family Grass (Poaceae)

Plant Characteristics Upright, warm-season, perennial bunchgrass 2 feet tall and wide; fine, narrow, gray-green leaves form a dense clump of arching, purple-tinted stems; spikes on stem tips above leaves are densely packed with small flowers followed by showy seed heads with three long, purple bristles (awns). Deer and rabbit resistant.

USDA Hardiness Zones 6a–10b

Bloom Period Spring and fall (April and October)

Growing Conditions Performs best in full sun and natural sandy, coarse, well-draining soil.

Forming dense clumps of stems with green-to-bluish-gray leaves topped with feathery spikes of reddish-purple seed heads, this drought-tolerant native provides a year-round colorful accent for landscapes. With soft-green textures in early spring, flaming seed heads dancing in the breeze all summer, and golden-brown stems in the winter, purple three-awn makes a dramatic border, groundcover, pattern, or mass planting. In a pollinator garden, bunchgrasses are larval hosts for moths and butterflies and provide nesting and overwintering habitat for bumblebees. This well-mannered bunchgrass self-seeds, especially with supplemental water, but it is not invasive and needs little or no maintenance beyond gently pulling out any untidy, dried seed stalks. The spiky seeds can stick in pet fur, but the grass can be trimmed in the summer before the seeds mature.

Provides nesting and overwinter habitat for bees; larval host for canyonland satyr (Cyllopsis pertepida) and grass skipper butterfly species (Hesperiidae).

Switchgrass

Scientific Name *Panicum virgatum*

Family Grass (Poaceae)

Plant Characteristics Warm-season perennial bunchgrass with dense columnar cluster of blue-green blades reaching 3–5 feet tall and 2–3 feet wide; flowers pink tinged, wind pollinated, stalks up to 3 feet above blades; seed heads reddish-purple. Deer, rabbit resistant.

USDA Hardiness Zones 4a–9b

Bloom Period Summer (August)

Growing Conditions Full sun to part shade; well-draining soil with moderate moisture.

With large clusters of blue-green leaves in the spring that turn golden brown in the fall, and with reddish-purple, airy seed heads, this large-scale bunchgrass provides an ornamental accent for four-seasons. Native from tall-grass prairies to transition regions, it is well adapted for Front Range habitats. Plant as a specimen accent, create a scattered pattern, a mass or screen planting, or use in naturalized areas. Leave clumps intact through the winter to protect overwintering insects, then cut back to the ground in early spring to remove thatch before new growth appears. Many cultivars have been selected for red leaves, size, and other ornamental features. Plants self-seed, though cultivars may produce mixed results.

Provides for butterflies and other small pollinators; game and songbirds birds eat the seeds; larval host for many butterflies species, including skippers, satyrs, and the common wood nymph (*Cercyonis pegala*).

Garden Plants for Butterflies

SHRUBS

1. **Antelope Bitterbrush** *(Purshia tridentata var. tridentata)*, pg. 57
2. **Chokecherry** *(Prunus virginiana)*, pg. 61
3. **Leadplant** *(Amorpha canascens)*, pg. 75
4. **Lewis Mock Orange** *(Philadelphus lewisii)*, pg. 77
5. **Mountain Ninebark** *(Physocarpus monogynus)*, pg. 79
6. **Mountainspray** *(Holodiscus discolor)*, pg. 81
7. **Rubber Rabbitbrush** *(Ericameria nauseosa)*, pg. 87
8. **White Spirea** *(Spiraea betulifolia)*, pg. 103

WILDFLOWERS

9. **Fireweed** *(Chamerion angustifolium)*, pg. 131
10. **Gayfeather** *(Liatris punctata)*, pg. 133
11. **Heartleaf Arnica** *(Arnica cordifolia)*, pg. 147
12. **Milkweeds** *(Asclepias spp.)*, pg. 115, 197
13. **Nettleleaf Giant Hyssop** *(Agastache urticifolia)*, pg. 157
14. **Prairie Coneflower** *(Ratibida columnifera)*, pg. 165
15. **Purple Aster** *(Dieteria canescens)*, pg. 169
16. **Three-nerved Goldenrod** *(Solidago velutina)*, pg. 213
17. **Western Wallflower** *(Erysimum capitatum)*, pg. 221
18. **Wild Bergamot** *(Monarda fistulosa)*, pg. 229

Garden Plants for Bees

SHRUBS
1. **Antelope Bitterbrush** (*Purshia tridentata* var. *tridentata*), pg. 57
2. **Cliffbush** (*Jamesia americana*), pg. 63
3. **Cliff Fendlerbush** (*Fendlera rupicola*), pg. 65
4. **Common Snowberry** (*Symphoricarpos albus* var. *laevigatus*), pg. 67
5. **Leadplant** (*Amorpha canascens*), pg. 75
6. **Mountain Ninebark** (*Physocarpus monogynus*), pg. 79
7. **Mountainspray** (*Holodiscus discolor*), pg. 81
8. **Rubber Rabbitbrush** (*Ericameria nauseosa*), pg. 87
9. **Shrubby Cinquefoil** (*Dasiphora fruticosa*), pg. 89
10. **Woods' Rose** (*Rosa woodsii*), pg. 105

WILDFLOWERS
11. **Blackeyed Susan** (*Rudbeckia hirta*), pg. 109
12. **Blanket Flower** (*Gaillardia aristata*), pg. 111
13. **Common Sunflower** (*Helianthus annuus*), pg. 121
14. **Golden Crownbeard** (*Verbesina encelioides*), pg. 137
15. **Hairy False Goldenaster** (*Heterotheca villosa*), pg. 143
16. **Milkweeds** (*Asclepias* spp.), pg. 115, 197
17. **Prairie Coneflower** (*Ratibida columnifera*), pg. 165
18. **Rocky Mountain Beeplant** (*Peritoma serrulata*), pg. 177
19. **Rocky Mountain Penstemon** (*Penstemon strictus*), pg. 183
20. **Rydberg's Penstemon** (*Penstemon rydbergii*), pg. 187
21. **Sulphur Flower Buckwheat** (*Eriogonum umbellatum*), pg. 211

Container Garden for Pollinators

WILDFLOWERS

1. **Black-eyed Susan** *(Rudbeckia hirta)*, pg. 109
2. **Colorado Blue Columbine** *(Aquilegia coerulea)*, pg. 117
3. **Orange Sneezeweed** *(Hymenoxys hoopseii)*, pg. 161
4. **Prairie Coneflower** *(Ratibida columnifera)*, pg. 165
5. **Silvery Lupine** *(Lupinus argenteus)*, pg. 201
6. **Wild Bergamot** *(Monarda fistulosa)*, pg. 229

Bird Food & Nesting Plants

TREES

COMMON NAME	SCIENTIFIC NAME
Colorado Blue Spruce pg. 41	Prunus virginiana
Gambel's Oak pg. 43	Quercus gambelii
Pinyon Pine pg. 45	Pinus edulis
Ponderosa Pine pg. 47	Pinus ponderosa
Quaking Aspen pg. 49	Populus tremuloides
Rocky Mountain Maple pg. 51	Acer glabrum

SHRUBS

COMMON NAME	SCIENTIFIC NAME
Blue Elderberry pg. 59	Frangula californica
Chokecherry pg. 61	Prunus virginiana
Golden Currant pg. 71	Ribes aureum
Gooseberry Currant pg. 73	Ribes montigenum
Red-osier Dogwood pg. 85	Cornus sericea
Smooth Sumac pg. 91	Rhus glabra
Thimbleberry pg. 95	Rubus parviflorus
Western Mountain Ash pg. 99	Sorbus sitchensis
Western Serviceberry pg. 101	Amelanchier alnifolia

WILDFLOWERS

COMMON NAME	SCIENTIFIC NAME
Common Sunflower pg. 121	Helianthus annuus

VINES

COMMON NAME	SCIENTIFIC NAME
Creeping Barberry pg. 237	Berberis repens

Hummingbird Plants

SHRUBS

COMMON NAME	SCIENTIFIC NAME
Gooseberry Currant pg. 73	*Ribes montigenum*
Leadplant pg. 75	*Amorpha canescens*
Twinberry Honeysuckle pg. 97	*Lonicera involucrata*

WILDFLOWERS

COMMON NAME	SCIENTIFIC NAME
Nettleleaf Giant Hyssop pg. 157	*Agastache urticifoliia*
Purple Locoweed pg. 171	*Oxytropis lambertii*
Rocky Mountain Beeplant pg. 177	*Peritoma serrulata*
Scarlet Globemallow pg. 189	*Sphaeralcea coccinea*
Skyrocket Gilia pg. 203	*Ipomopsis aggregata*
Western Red Columbine pg. 217	*Aquilegia formosa*
Wild Bergamot pg. 229	*Monarda fistulosa*

Larval Host List (By Butterfly/Moth Species)

Plants marked with an asterisk (*) are not featured in this book.

BUTTERFLIES

American Lady
(*Vanessa virginiensis*)

Pearly Everlasting, pg. 163
(*Anaphalis margaritacea*)

Silver Sage Wormwood, pg. 245
(*Artemisia ludoviciana*)

Threadleaf Groundsel*
(*Senecio flaccidus*)

American Snout
(*Libytheana carinenta*)

Netleaf Hackberry*
(*Celtis reticulata*)

Arizona Sister
(*Adelpha eulalia*)

Oaks, pg. 43
(*Quercus* spp.)

Black Swallowtail
(*Papilio polyxenes*)

Parsley family*
(Apiaceae)

Bordered Patch
(*Chlosyne lacinia*)

Blanket Flower, pg. 111
(*Gaillardia aristata*)

Golden Crownbeard, pg. 137
(*Verbesina encelioides*)

Sunflowers, pg. 121
(*Helianthus* spp.)

Emperor butterflies
(*Apaturinae* spp.)

Hackberry*
(*Celtis* spp.)

Gray Hairstreak
(*Strymon melinus*)

Buckwheats, pg. 211
(*Eriogonum* spp.)

Desert Globemallow*
(*Sphaeralcea ambigua*)

Leadplant, pg. 75
(*Amorpha canescens*)

Legume family,
pgs. 75, 141, 153, 171, 173, 201, 219, 227
(Fabaceae)

Mallow family,
pgs. 159, 189, 209
(Malvaceae)

Western Serviceberry, pg. 101
(*Amelanchier alnifolia*)

Juniper Hairstreak
(*Callophrys gryneus*)

Junipers*
(*Juniperus* spp.)

Lupine Blue
(*Plebejus lupini*)

Sulphur Flower Buckwheat, pg. 211
(*Eriogonum umbellatum*)

Monarch, Queen
(*Danaus plexippus, D. gilippus*)

Milkweeds, pgs. 115, 197
(*Asclepias* spp.)

Mourning Cloak
(*Nymphalis antiopa*)

Cottonwoods & Aspens,
pg. 49
(*Populus* spp.)

Elm*
(*Ulmus* spp.)

Rocky Mountain Maple,
pg. 51
(*Acer glabrum*)

Willows*
(*Salix* spp.)

Painted Lady
(*Vanessa cardui*)

Common Sunflower, pg. 121
(*Helianthus annuus*)

Common Yarrow, pg. 123
(*Achillea millefolium*)

Legume family,
pgs. 75, 141, 153, 171,
173, 201, 219, 227
(Fabaceae)

Pearly Everlasting, pg. 163
(*Anaphalis margaritacea*)

Scarlet Globemallow, pg. 189
(*Sphaeralcea coccinea*)

Thistles*
(*Cirsium* spp.)

Pale Swallowtail
(*Papilio eurymedon*)

Chokecherry, pg. 61
(*Prunus virginiana*)

Pearl Crescent
(*Phyciodes tharos*)

Smooth Blue Aster, pg. 205
(*Symphyotrichum laeve*)

White Heath Aster, pg. 225
(*Symphyotrichum ericoides*)

Sagebrush Checkerspot
(*Chlosyne acastus*)

Aster family, pg. 87, 93, 109,
111, 119, 121, 123, 133, 137,
139, 143, 147, 161, 163, 165,
169, 179, 191, 193, 205, 213,
225, 245
(Asteraceae)

Rubber Rabbitbrush,
pg. 87
(*Ericameria nauseosa*)

Southern Dogface
(*Zerene cesonia*)

False Indigo*
(*Amorpha fruticosa*)

Prairie-clovers, pgs. 173, 227
(Dalea)

Texas Crescent
(*Anthanassa texana*)

Honeysuckle family,
pgs. 67, 97
(Caprifoliaceae)

Two-Tailed Swallowtail
(*Papilio multicaudata*)

Chokecherry, pg. 61
(*Prunus virginiana*)

Western Hop Tree*
(*Ptelea crenulata*)

Velvet Ash*
(*Fraxinus velutina*)

Variegated Fritillary
(*Euptoieta claudia*)

Blue Flax, pg. 113
(*Linum lewisii*)

Passion Vine*
(*Passiflora* spp.)

Violets, pg. 149
(*Viola* spp.)

Larval Host List (continued)

BUTTERFLIES (continued)

Western Tiger Swallowtail
(*Papilio rutulus*)

Chokecherry p. 61
(*Prunus virginiana*)

Cottonwoods & Aspens, pg. 49
(*Populus* spp.)

Velvet Ash*
(*Fraxinus velutina*)

Willows*
(*Salix* spp.)

MOTHS

Columbia Silkmoth
(*Hyalophora columbia*)

Alderleaf Mountain Mahogany, pg. 55
(*Cercocarpus montanus*)

Chokecherry p. 61
(*Prunus virginiana*)

Willows*
(*Salix* spp.)

Woods' Rose, pg. 105
(*Rosa woodsii*)

Hawkmoths
(*Sphingidae* spp.)

Pale Wolfberry*
(*Lycium pallidum*)

Potato/tomato family*
(Solanaceae)

White-Lined Sphinx Moth
(*Hyles lineata*)

Evening Primroses, pgs. 215
(*Oenothera* spp.)

Giant Four O'Clock*
(*Mirabilis gigantea*)

Potato/tomato family*
(Solanaceae)

Retail Sources of Rocky Mountain Native Seeds & Plants

COLORADO SOURCES AND PLANT SALES

High Plains Environmental Center Native Plant Nursery
suburbitat.org

Loveland, CO

Online lists of native plant sources
denveraudubon.org/where-to-find-co-native-plants
frontrange.wildones.org/resources/purchase-native-plants

NEW MEXICO

High Country Gardens
highcountrygardens.com

Online only–all states

Plants of the Southwest
plantsofthesouthwest.com

3095 Agua Fria Street
Santa Fe, NM 87507

WYOMING

Piney Island Native Plants
pineyislandnatives.com
email: pineyislandnativeplants@gmail.com

P.O. Box 7002
Sheridan, WY 82801
(831) 659-1990

Wyoming Plant Company
Retail store only

358 South Ash Street
Casper, WY 82601
(307) 262-2963

Online lists of native plant sources
rockies.audubon.org/habitat-hero/resources/native-plant-retailers

Native Plant Societies

COLORADO NATIVE PLANT SOCIETY
conps.org

NATIVE PLANT SOCIETY OF NEW MEXICO
npsnm.org

UTAH NATIVE PLANT SOCIETY
unps.org

WYOMING NATIVE PLANT SOCIETY
wynps.org

Botanical Gardens & Arboretums

COLORADO

Betty Ford Alpine Botanical Garden
bettyfordalpinegardens.org

522 S. Frontage Road E.
Vail, CO 81657
(909) 476-0103

Denver Botanical Gardens
botanicgardens.org

1007 York Street
Denver, CO 80206
(720) 865-3500

Denver Botanical Gardens Chatfield Farms
botanicgardens.org/chatfield-farms

8500 W. Deer Creek Canyon Road
Littleton, CO 80128
(720) 865-3500

The Gardens on Spring Creek
fcgov.com/gardens

2145 Central Avenue
Fort Collins, CO 80526

Montrose Botanic Gardens
montrosegardens.org

1800 Pavilion Drive
Montrose, CO 81401

Shambhala Botanic Gardens

4921 County Road 68-C
Red Feather Lakes, CO 80545

Yampa River Botanic Park
yampariverbotanicpark.org

1000 Pamela Lane
Steamboat Springs, CO 80477

MONTANA

Conservation Garden Park
conservationgardenpark.org

8275 S. 1300th W.
West Jordan, UT 84088
(801) 256-4400

Ogden Botanical Gardens
extension.usu.edu/ogdenbotanicalgardens

1750 Monroe Boulevard
Ogden, UT 84401

Red Butte Botanical Garden
redbuttegarden.org

300 Wakara Way
Salt Lake City, UT 84108
(801) 585-0556

State of Montana Arboretum
email: arboretum@umontana.edu
umt.edu/arboretum

32 Campus Drive
Missoula, MT 59812
(406) 243-5579

Tizer Botanic Gardens & Arboretum
email: info@tizergardens.com
tizergardens.com

38 Tizer Lake Road
Jefferson City, MT 59638
(406) 933-8789

USU Botanical Center
extension.usu.edu/botanicalcenter

80 E. 725 S. Sego Lily Drive
Kaysville, UT 84037

WYOMING

Cheyenne Botanical Gardens
botanic.org

710 S. Lions Park Drive
Cheyenne, WY 82001
(307) 637-6458

Index

A
Acer glabrum, 26–27, 51
Achillea millefolium, 30–31, 123
Achnatherum hymenoides, 36–37, 255
Agastache urticifolia, 32–33, 157
Alderleaf Mountain Mahogany, 26–27, 55
Alkali Sacaton, 36–37, 253
Amelanchier alnifolia, 28–29, 101
Amorpha canescens, 26–27, 75
Anaphalis margaritacea, 32–33, 163
Anemone multifida, 30–31, 125
Antelope Bitterbush, 26–27, 57
Aquilegia chrysantha, 30–31, 135
Aquilegia coerulea, 30–31, 117
Aquilegia formosa, 34–35, 217
Arctostaphylos uva-ursi, 36–37, 239
Aristida purpurea, 36–37, 257
Arnica cordifolia, 30–31, 147
Artemisia ludoviciana, 36–37, 245
Asclepias speciosa, 34–35, 197
Asclepias tuberosa, 28–29, 115
Astragalus crassicarpus, 30–31, 141

B
Berberis repens, 36–37, 237
Black-eyed Susan, 28–29, 109
Blanket Flower, 28–29, 111
Blue Elderberry, 26–27, 59
Blue Flax, 28–29, 113
Bunchberry, 34–35, 235
Butterfly Milkweed, 28–29, 115

C
Camassia quamash, 32–33, 175
Campanula rotundifolia, 30–31, 145
Cerocarpus montanus, 26–27, 55
Chamerion angustifolium, 30–31, 131
Chokecherry, 26–27, 61
Clematis ligusticifolia, 36–37, 249
Cliffbush, 26–27, 63
Cliff Fendlerbush, 26–27, 65
Colorado Blue Columbine, 30–31, 117
Colorado Blue Spruce, 26–27, 41
Colorado (Pinque) Rubberweed, 30–31, 119
Common Snowberry, 26–27, 67
Common Sunflower, 30–31, 121
Common Yarrow, 30–31, 123
Cornus canadensis, 34–35, 235
Cornus sericea, 28–29, 85
Creeping Barberry, 36–37, 237
Cutleaf Anemone, 30–31, 125

D
Dalea candida, 34–35, 227
Dalea purpurea, 32–33, 173
Dasiphora fruticosa, 28–29, 89
Delphinium nuttallianum, 30–31, 129
Desert Prince's Plume, 30–31, 127
Dieteria canescens, 32–33, 169
Dwarf Larkspur, 30–31, 129

E
Ericameria nauseosa, 28–29, 87
Erigeron speciosus, 32–33, 191
Erigonum umbellatum, 34–35, 211
Erysimum capitatum, 34–35, 221

F
Fendlera rupicola, 26–27, 65
Fireweed, 30–31, 131
Fragrant Sumac, 26–27, 69

G
Gaillardia aristata, 28–29, 111
Gambel's Oak, 26–27, 43
Gayfeather, 30–31, 133
Geranium viscosissimum, 34–35, 207
Golden Columbine, 30–31, 135
Golden Crownbeard, 30–31, 137
Golden Currant, 26–27, 71
Gooseberry Currant, 26–27, 73
Greenthread, 30–31, 139
Groundplum Milkvetch, 30–31, 141
Gutierrezia sarothrae, 28–29, 93

H
Hairy False Goldenaster, 30–31, 143
Harebell, 30–31, 145
Heartleaf Arnica, 30–31, 147
Hedysarum occidentale, 34–35, 219
Helianthus annuus, 30–31, 121
Heliomeris multiflora, 32–33, 193
Heterotheca villosa, 30–31, 143
Holodiscus discolor (dumosus), 28–29, 81
Hooked-spur Blue Violet, 30–31, 149
Hymenoxys hoopesii, 32–33, 161
Hymenoxys richardsonii, 30–31, 119

I
Iliamana rivularis, 34–35, 209
Indian Ricegrass, 36–37, 255
Ipomopsis arggregata, 34–35, 203
Iris missouriensis, 32–33, 181

J
Jamesia americana, 26–27, 63

K
Kinnikinnick, Bearberry, 36–37, 239

L
Lanceleaf Stonecrop, 36–37, 241
Leadplant, 26–27, 75
Lewis Mock Orange, 28–29, 77
Liatris punctata, 30–31, 133
Linum lewisii, 28–29, 113
Lonicera involucrata, 28–29, 97
Lupinus argenteus, 34–35, 201

M
Mertensia lanceolata, 30–31, 155
Monarda fistulosa, 34–35, 229
Mountain Blue-eyed Grass, 30–31, 151
Mountain Golden Banner, 30–31, 153
Mountain Ninebark, 28–29, 79
Mountainspray, 28–29, 81

N
Narrowleaf Bluebells, 30–31, 155
Nettleleaf Giant Hyssop, 32–33, 157
New Mexico Checkermallow, 32–33, 159

O
Oenothera cespitosa, 34–35, 215
Orange Sneezeweed, 32–33, 161
Oxytropis lambertii, 32–33, 171

P
Packera streptanthifolia, 32–33, 179
Panicum virgatum, 36–37, 259
Parthenocissus vitazea, 36–37, 247
Pearly Everlasting, 32–33, 163
Penstemon rydbergii, 32–33, 187
Penstemon segundiflorus, 34–35, 199
Penstemon strictus, 32–33, 183
Penstemon whippleanus, 34–35, 223
Peritoma lutea, 34–35, 231
Peritoma serrulata, 32–33, 177
Philadelphus lewisii, 28–29, 77
Phlox multiflora, 32–33, 185
Physocarpus monogynus, 28–29, 79
Picea pungens, 26–27, 41
Pinus edulis, 26–27, 45
Pinus ponderosa, 26–27, 47
Pinyon Pine, 26–27, 45
Polemonium pulcherrimum, 32–33, 195
Ponderosa Pine, 26–27, 47
Populus tremuloides, 26–27, 49
Prairie Coneflower, 32–33, 165
Prairie Spiderwort, 32–33, 167

Prunella vulgaris, 36–37, 243
Prunus virginiana, 26–27, 61
Purple Aster, 32–33, 169
Purple Locoweed, 32–33, 171
Purple Prairie-clover, 32–33, 173
Purple Three-awn, 36–37, 257
Purshia tridentata var. *tridentata,* 26–27, 57

Q
Quaking Aspen, 26–27, 49
Quamash, 32–33, 175
Quercus gambelii, 26–27, 43

R
Ratibida columnifera, 32–33, 165
Red Elderberry, 28–29, 83
Red-osier Dogwood, 28–29, 85
Rhus aromatica (tribolata), 26–27, 69
Rhus glabra, 28–29, 91
Ribes aureum, 26–27, 71
Ribes montigenium, 26–27, 73
Rocky Mountain Beeplant, 32–33, 177
Rocky Mountain Groundsel, 32–33, 179
Rocky Mountain Iris, 32–33, 181
Rocky Mountain Maple, 26–27, 51
Rocky Mountain Penstemon, 32–33, 183
Rocky Mountain Phlox, 32–33, 185
Rosa woodsii, 28–29, 105
Rubber Rabbitbrush, 28–29, 87
Rubus parviflorus, 28–29, 95
Rudbeckia hirta, 28–29, 109
Rydberg's Penstemon, 32–33, 187

S
Sambucus nigra ssp. *cerulea,* 26–27, 59
Sambucus racemosa, 28–29, 83
Scarlet Globemallow, 32–33, 189
Sedum lanceolatum, 36–37, 241
Self-heal, 36–37, 243
Showy Fleabane, 32–33, 191
Showy Goldeneye, 32–33, 193
Showy Jacob's Ladder, 32–33, 195
Showy Milkweed, 34–35, 197
Shrubby Cinquefoil, 28–29, 89
Sidalcea neomexicana, 32–33, 159
Sidebells Penstemon, 34–35, 199
Silver Sage Wormwood, 36–37, 245
Silvery Lupine, 34–35, 201
Sisyrinchium montanum, 30–31, 151
Skyrocket Gilia, 34–35, 203
Smooth Blue Aster, 34–35, 205
Smooth Sumac, 28–29, 91
Snakeweed, Broomweed, 28–29, 93
Solidago velutina, 34–35, 213
Sorbus sitchensis, 28–29, 99
Sphaeralcea coccinea, 32–33, 189

Spiraea betulifolia, 28–29, 103
Sporobolus airoides, 36–37, 253
Stanleya pinnata, 30–31, 127
Sticky Geranium, 34–35, 207
Streambank Wild Hollycock, 34–35, 209
Sulphur Flower Buckwheat, 34–35, 211
Switchgrass, 36–37, 259
Symphoricarpos albus var. *laevigatus*, 26–27, 67
Symphyotrichum ericoides, 34–35, 225
Symphyotrichum laeve, 34–35, 205

T
Thelesperma filifolium, 30–31, 139
Thermopsis montana, 30–31, 153
Thicket Creeper, 36–37, 247
Thimbleberry, 28–29, 95
Three-nerved Goldenrod, 34–35, 213
Tradescantia occidentalis, 32–33, 167
Tufted Evening Primrose, 34–35, 215
Twinberry Honeysuckle, 28–29, 97

V
Verbesina encelioides, 30–31, 137
Viola adunca, 30–31, 149

W
Western Mountain Ash, 28–29, 99
Western Red Columbine, 34–35, 217
Western Serviceberry, 28–29, 101
Western Sweetvetch, 34–35, 219
Western Virgin's Bower, 36–37, 249
Western Wallflower, 34–35, 221
Whipple's Penstemon, 34–35, 223
White Heath Aster, 34–35, 225
White Prairie-clover, 34–35, 227
White Spirea, 28–29, 103
Wild Bergamot, 34–35, 229
Wood's Rose, 28–29, 105

Y
Yellow Beeplant, 34–35, 231

Photo Credits

Interior photos by George Oxford Miller except as noted below. All photos copyright of their respective photographers.
Carole Price: 280

These images are licensed under the CC0 1.0 Universal (CC0 1.0) Public Domain Dedication license, which is available at https://creativecommons.org/publicdomain/zero/1.0/ or licensed under Public Domain Mark 1.0, which is available at https://creativecommons.org/publicdomain/mark/1.0/: **Patrick Alexander:** 119, 171, 185, 252, 255, 259; **Jacob W. Frank/NPS:** 124; **Peter Garber:** 105; **Mike Goad:** 109; **Robb Hannawacker:** 169, 217, 269 (sagebrush checkerspot butterfly and larva); **John Kenny:** 225; **Shane Johnson:** 99, 209; **Braden J. Judson:** 125; **Tom Koerner/USFWS:** 177, 231; **Craig Martin:** 63, 79, 161; **NPS/S. Zenner/Grand Teton National Park:** 128; **Dom Paulo:** 151; **Jesse Rorabaugh:** 193; **Erik Schiff:** 91; **ALAN SCHMIERER:** 100; **Patrick Sowers:** 57; **Erin Springinotic:** 89; **Kate E Tillotson:** 141; **Yellowstone National Park/NPS/Neal Herbert:** 181

These images are licensed under the Attribution 2.0 Generic (CC BY 2.0) license, which is available at https://creativecommons.org/licenses/by/2.0/: **aecole2010:** 75, no modifications, original image at https://www.flickr.com/photos/aecole/42612920585/, 173, no modifications, original image at https://www.flickr.com/photos/aecole/29646402988/; **Theo Arnold:** 269 (Texas crescent butterfly), https://www.flickr.com/photos/92829839@N02/8475507604/; **Cataloging Nature:** 268 (emperor larva), https://www.flickr.com/photos/kz_yb/36839208312/; **Jacob W. Frank/RMNP:** 199, no modifications, original image at https://www.flickr.com/photos/rockynps/14803441150/; **Judy Gallagher:** 90, no modifications, original image at https://www.flickr.com/photos/52450054@N04/50668097881/; **John Game:** 149, no modifications, original image at https://www.flickr.com/photos/47945928@N02/4159464930 5/; **sodai gomi:** 211, no modifications, original image at https://www.flickr.com/photos/sodaigomi/28001464237/; **JKehoe:** 81, no modifications, original image at https://www.flickr.com/photos/johnjkehoe_photography/17958275140/; **Steve Jurvetson:** 23 (tiger moth), no modifications, original image at https://commons.wikimedia.org/wiki/File:Pyrrharctia_isabella.jpg; **Tom Koerner/USFWS:** 101, no modifications, original image at https://www.flickr.com/photos/usfwsmtnprairie/35814922260/; **Paul Asman and Jill Lenoble:** 187, no modifications, original image at https://www.flickr.com/photos/pauljill/5232998455 0/; **Clinton & Charles Robertson:** 268 (bordered patch larva), no modifications, original image at https://www.flickr.com/photos/dad_and_clint/558690732/; **Katja Schulz:** 156, no modifications, original image at https://www.flickr.com/photos/treegrow/14891662378/; **B Smith:** 268 (gray hairstreak larva), no modifications, original image at https://www.flickr.com/photos/twiztedminds/50355917511/; **Forest and Kim Starr:** 120, no modifications, original image at https://www.flickr.com/photos/starr-environmental/25435860397/, 137, no modifications, original image at https://www.flickr.com/photos/starr-environmental/25242367946/; **Peter Stevens:** 98, no modifications, original image at https://www.flickr.com/photos/nordique/3751126652/; **Andrey Zharkikh:** 54, no modifications, original image at https://www.flickr.com/photos/zharkikh/17271811246/, 65, no modifications, original image at https://www.flickr.com/photos/zharkikh/19361188254/, 73, no modifications, original image at https://www.flickr.com/photos/zharkikh/6428072053/, 92, no modifications, original image at https://www.flickr.com/photos/zharkikh/51435776340/, 157, no modifications, original image at https://www.flickr.com/photos/zharkikh/6425731535/, 241, no modifications, original image at https://www.flickr.com/photos/zharkikh/52686995357/

These images are licensed under the Attribution 4.0 International (CC BY 4.0) license, which is available at https://creativecommons.org/licenses/by/4.0/: **John Abrams:** 229, no modifications, original image at https://www.inaturalist.org/photos/142136371/; **Matt Berger:** 51, no modifications, original image at https://www.inaturalist.org/photos/232415873/, 207, no modifications, original image at https://www.inaturalist.org/photos/140325756/; **Jeff Birek:** 205, no modifications, original image at https://www.inaturalist.org/photos/316186708/; **Coral Ridge Studio-Jay Brasher:** 249, no modifications, original image at https://www.inaturalist.org/photos/167190738/; **Patrick Delhalt:** 270 (Columbia silkmoth larva), no modifications, original image at https://www.inaturalist.org/photos/314999085/; **desertnaturalist:** 113, no modifications, original image at https://www.inaturalist.org/photos/88438574/; **Jonathan Eisen:** 213, no modifications, original image at https://www.inaturalist.org/photos/32937834/; **evangrimes:** 139, no modifications, original image at https://www.inaturalist.org/photos/145019327/; **Nolan Exe:** 195, no modifications, original image at https://www.inaturalist.org/photos/319522032/, 219, no modifications, original image at https://www.inaturalist.org/photos/150393668/; **Rob Foster:** 235, no modifications, original image at https://www.inaturalist.org/photos/77909231/; **Laura Gaudette:** 268 (juniper hairstreak larva), no modifications, original image at https://www.inaturalist.org/photos/232027972/; **Darrin Gobble:** 129, no modifications, original image at https://www.inaturalist.org/photos/276584289/; **john_hall:** 69, no modifications, original image at https://www.inaturalist.org/photos/187470923/; **Anders Hastings:** 155, no modifications, original image at https://www.inaturalist.org/photos/297175847/; **icosahedron:** 245, no modifications, original image at https://www.inaturalist.org/photos/18198924/; **jeffnoh:** 268 (lupine blue butterfly), no modifications, original image at https://www.inaturalist.org/photos/330265798/; **CK Kelly:** 121, no modifications, original image at https://www.inaturalist.org/photos/233549950/; **Daniel Kennedy:** 201, no modifications, original image at https://www.inaturalist.org/photos/268353104/; **Sam Kieschnick:** 215, no modifications, original image at https://www.inaturalist.org/photos/207983870/; **Mary Krieger:** 227, no modifications, original image at https://www.inaturalist.org/photos/9212180/; **LBuffum:** 45, no modifications, original image at https://www.inaturalist.org/photos/54384975/; **My-Lan Le:** 47, no modifications, original image at https://www.inaturalist.org/photos/279608938/; **Don Loarie:** 223, no modifications, original image at https://www.inaturalist.org/photos/4557080/; **Scott Loarie:** 260 (Erysimum capitatum inset), no modifications, original image at https://www.inaturalist.org/photos/8544496/; **Doug Macaulay:** 133, no modifications, original image at https://www.inaturalist.org/photos/4157571/; **Steve Matson:** 179, no modifications, original image at https://www.inaturalist.org/photos/94058798/; **Paul McClellan:** 87, no modifications, original image at https://www.inaturalist.org/photos/229543083/; **David McCorquodale:** 243, no modifications, original image at https://www.inaturalist.org/photos/316095968/; **Melissa McMasters:** 253, no modifications, original image at https://www.inaturalist.org/photos/42646702/; **Andrew Meeds:** 268 (American snout larva), no modifications, original image at https://www.inaturalist.org/photos/175644394/; **LJ Moore-McClelland:** 269 (pale swallowtail larva), no modifications, original image at https://www.inaturalist.org/photos/317079149/; **nmoorhatch:** 189, no modifications, original image at https://www.inaturalist.org/photos/316417989/; **Tanya Riseman:** 95, no modifications, original image at https://www.inaturalist.org/photos/109034554/; **Rick Robb:** 247, no modifications, original image at https://www.inaturalist.org/photos/48570460/; **Liz Smith:** 83, no modifications, original image at https://www.inaturalist.org/photos/46628707/; **Rachel Stringham:** 159, no modifications, original image at https://www.inaturalist.org/photos/85876871/; **Ken-ichi Ueda:** 97, no modifications, original image at https://www.inaturalist.org/photos/119321742/; **Mathew Zappa:** 143, no modifications, original image at https://www.inaturalist.org/photos/208880845/, 268 (Arizona sister larva), no modifications, original image at https://www.inaturalist.org/photos/183914980/

Images used under license from shutterstock.com.
Achkin: 237; **Toporovska Alla:** 71; **AnaGoncalves93:** 268 (American lady larva); **Judith Andrews:** 191; **avkost:** 67; **Gerry Bishop:** 268 (American lady butterfly); **Randy Bjorklund:** 268 (American snout butterfly); **Kseniya Bogdanova:** 40; **Donna Bollenbach:** 269 (pearl crescent butterfly); **Jennifer Bosvert:** 197; **B Brown:** 50; **Charles Lemar Brown:** 138; **Katja Bruckner:** 134; **Steve Byland:** 22 (Arizona sister); **goran cakmazovic:** 16; **carolinacanas:** 261 (driftwood background); **ccpixx photography:** 270 (five-spotted hawkmoth larva); **Danica Chang:** 6; **Chris Lawrence Travel:** 258; **CinemaPhoto:** 246; **William Cushman:** 13; **Dee Carpenter Originals:** 61; **Danita Delimont:** 135, 203, 267; **D.Heesbeen:** 145; **DMC-13:** 167; **Le Do:** 22 (monarch inset); **Ken Donaldson:** 117; **Melinda Fawver:** 268 (juniper hairstreak butterfly); **Dmitry Fch:** 269 (painted lady larva); **Katie Flenker:** 256; **ForestSeasons:** 46; **Dominic Gentilcore PhD:** 43; **J.J. Gouin:** 115; **guaryderey:** 257; **Jacob Hamblin:** 270 (western tiger swallowtail larva); **Keith Hider:** 221; **h.jack:** 239; **Susan Hodgson:** 17, 183; **Brett Hondow:** 269 (pearl crescent larva); **hunkir:** 11; **I.lika:** 59; **Cristina Ionescu:** 15; **Jiujiuer:** 254; **Tiffany K:** 23 (police car moth); **Nikolay Kurzenko:** 74; **kzww:** 21 (bumble bee inset); **Akash Lanjekar:** 269 (monarch larva); **LapailrKrapai:** 103; **Mariskan foto:** 131; **MassimilianoPaolino:** 269 (mourning cloak larva); **Micheal G McKinne:** 269 (variegated fritillary butterfly); **MelaniWright:** 93; **meunierd:** 202; **M. Leonard Photography:** 55; **Sari ONeal:** 269 (variegated fritillary larva), 270 (five-spotted hawkmoth); **Marci Paravia:** 163; **Tom Reichner:** 49; **Leena Robinson:** 114, 165, 268 (emperor butterfly); **Paul Roedding:** 85; **Scenic Corner:** 127; **Stefan Schug:** 96; **SeDmi:** 265 (soil background); **Annette Shaff:** 147; **Sigur:** 238; **Slick.Root:** 111; **Christine Stafford:** 269 (two-tailed swallowtail larva); **Mike Truchon:** 41; **Bryony van der Merwe:** 153; **Jonas Vegele:** 174; **Jim and Lynne Weber:** 23 (Columbia silkmoth), 123, 270 (Columbia silkmoth butterfly); **Don Williamson:** 269 (pale swallowtail butterfly); **Wingman Photography:** 22 (black swallowtail), 268 (bordered patch butterfly); **Bety X:** 175; **Sean Xu:** 10; **Nikki Yancey:** 42, 44, 77

Notes

The Story of AdventureKEEN

We are an independent nature and outdoor activity publisher. Our founding dates back more than 40 years, guided then and now by our love of being in the woods and on the water, by our passion for reading and books, and by the sense of wonder and discovery made possible by spending time recreating outdoors in beautiful places.

It is our mission to share that wonder and fun with our readers, especially with those who haven't yet experienced all the physical and mental health benefits that nature and outdoor activity can bring.

In addition, we strive to teach about responsible recreation so that the natural resources and habitats we cherish and rely upon will be available for future generations.

We are a small team deeply rooted in the places where we live and work. We have been shaped by our communities of origin—primarily Birmingham, Alabama; Cincinnati, Ohio; and the northern suburbs of Minneapolis, Minnesota. Drawing on the decades of experience of our staff and our awareness of the industry, the marketplace, and the world at large, we have shaped a unique vision and mission for a company that serves our readers and authors.

We hope to meet you out on the trail someday.

#bewellbeoutdoors

About the Author

George Oxford Miller (1943-2024) was a botanist, nature photographer, environmental journalist, and near-lifelong resident of the West. He lived in California, Texas, Arizona, and New Mexico. He served as president and was a lifetime member of the Albuquerque chapter of the Native Plant Society of New Mexico.

George earned his master's degree in zoology and botany from the University of Texas at Austin. He was the author of 15 guidebooks to the West. George's books for Adventure Publications include *Native Plant Gardening for Birds, Bees & Butterflies: Southwest, The Rocky Mountain Plant Guide,* and seven wildflower quick guides. He also wrote the "Plant of the Month" column for *New Mexico Magazine.* His wildflower website, WildflowersNM.com, describes more than 700 species with photos and identification tips. His knowledge and kindness were gifts to all.